Interview Success

Interview Success

Mike Culley C.Psychol. AFBPsS
www.interviewsuccess.uk

First Edition 2023

To Jane

Contents

Introduction

Thank you for choosing this book. My aim is that, within it, you will find many ideas that can help you to improve your interview technique, and so greatly enhance your chances of success.

The ideas presented here are some of those gained through my experience on both sides of the interview process – undertaking selection and interviews for organisations and coaching individuals for their own interviews.

Interviews are challenging and, obviously, competitive - you need ways to create powerful individualised interview responses that can help you to stand out from the crowd, and to achieve the confident and positive mindset necessary for success.

Having conducted hundreds of interviews, I have seen a remarkable variety of applicants and approaches to them. Sometimes, the quality and authenticity of the applicant's answers, combined with the way they confidently presented themselves, meant that we felt confident that the applicant would perform well in the role.

However, applicants' preparation and presentation is not always that good - I have also been involved in many interviews where the interviewees lack of preparation, insight, and overall awareness was very noticeable and damaged their chances of success. Make sure that you are not one of these...

Naturally, no book can ever replace one-to-one live coaching, which is personalised to both you and the position that you are applying for, and which delivers individualised feedback to help you really develop your interview skills. However, I have tried to ensure that there are many fresh ideas that you can use to help you, whether you are seeking a promotion within your current organisation, a new job, or a whole new career.

Now many people preparing for an interview naturally focus exclusively upon the possible questions and good answers to them, but there are other elements of interview technique that can be just as important. These include projecting confidence, demonstrating positive body language, or even aspects of prior research into the interviewer's organisation. These are factors that I find many people don't think about often enough, so we will be looking at those.

Every person going for an interview is different. Every organisation they are applying to is different. Every position within that organisation is different. Every interviewer is different, and so on… There are countless possible permutations of people and situation… Naturally this means there isn't one ideal answer for every interview situation, so we will explore not only some great answers, but the underlying principles that could help you adapt your answers depending on the situation. By understanding the principles, you will be able to deliver an effective individualised response, for that particular interview, at that particular time.

We will also help you avoid some of the many, many problems and traps that people so often fall into at their interview that can ruin their chances.

Just as there is no single ideal answer to an interview question, neither are there absolute rules for interviews. To give an example, one of the often-quoted suggestions for interview technique concerns when the interviewer might ask you to tell them something about yourself – a classic opening question.

Traditionally you are told that it is best to avoid talking about religion or politics at this point – advice which is sound most of the time. However, if you are going for a position as a union leader or perhaps a church minister, discussion of politics or religion may be absolutely relevant - indeed probably essential. You need to be aware and adapt to your own interview scenario.

Now, most discussions of interviews assume that interviews are held in a completely unbiased environment where people will make up their minds about you and your suitability logically, dispassionately and based purely on the quality of your answers. Other human factors such as personality, and the liking, or otherwise, of the interviewer for the interviewee won't come into the decision-making process.

Of course, most organisations would say that this is how they work, but this goes against thousands of years of human nature. Yes, interviews should be fair, but human biases will usually sneak through and influence people in ways that override any intentions to be entirely unemotional about the decision - even if we believe that this is not the case. So, although no two interviews are the same, the common factor is that there are (currently, mostly) human beings conducting them. One of the secrets of interview success is being aware and working with these human factors – possibly even using them to your advantage.

You should also be aware that, however well prepared as you may be, you will never have a 100% chance of interview success. There are too many imponderables – you don't know who you are up against for the post. You often don't know, despite the job description etc, exactly what they are really looking for. So, we can't be certain, but we can work to tip the balance more in your favour. Each improvement to your interview technique – whether in quality of answers, or mindset and presence - will increase your chances.

Sometimes you might even go for an interview and realise part way through that the panel is just going through the motions. Perhaps they already appear to have someone lined up for the post, but because of policy they still needed to advertise it more widely. Is that fair, or right? No, of course it isn't. But it does occur and if it should happen to you, do remember that you have a choice. You could be tempted to ease off and just go through the motions yourself, putting little effort into the interview, but instead, how about using the interview as a chance to develop your interview skills for the next time? Rather than just answering, crank your interview focus up a notch and deliver your best answers. Perhaps even try things out – play a little with your responses. Gain confidence through increased real interview experience and use the opportunity to hear how your answers sound delivered in the heat of an actual interview. No practice will ever quite be as good as the real thing, so use the interview constructively as an opportunity, not a waste of time.

And, you never know - as well as building your interview experience and confidence it is not unknown for that already lined-up person for a position to be so laid back and overconfident that they deliver a poor interview. I have encountered several situations like this, where an outside applicant let off the leash by circumstances has been so effective and fresh in their answers that they get the position over the individual that had been expected to get it.

Also, it also can occur that a while after interview another position becomes available in the organisation and the interviewer has been so impressed by an applicant that they contact them about this new opening. So, it is worth always giving each interview your very best.

Every interview is an opportunity to either succeed or increase your chances to do so next time.

You will find more free resources to aid your interview performance at my website: **www.interviewsuccess.uk**

So now, let's start to explore interviews, and how to succeed at them...

Types of Interviews

Firstly, if you are less experienced at being interviewed, you may be unaware of the different types of interviews you could encounter, so let's look at some of the most common types.

There are quite a few varieties, but there is always likely to be a considerable overlap between them. After all, at the end of the day, whatever type of interview you encounter, the interviewer will want to know pretty much the same things about you – what you are good at, what you aren't, your background, work ethic and what skills and experience you will be bringing to the organisation. It's just how they get at them that will vary.

Where there is more than one interviewer, the panel will usually consist of a mix of individuals, each there for a different reason, and so looking for different aspects. Frequently there are three people on the interview panel, and in his case the lead interviewer may be a senior leader who is effectively the one making the final hiring decision, and whose department or team you would be joining. A second interviewer with them may be someone acting as a technical expert to check your experience, knowledge, and skills in a key area of the role. The third person will then often be someone from the HR Department, there to oversee the interview and to make sure it is conducted properly and fairly.

The Formal/Traditional Interview

First off, we have the formal or traditional interview, the classic type with you and the interviewers face to face in a room (or online) while they ask you a range of questions.

In the traditional interview you will usually be asked various questions based around topics such as your strengths and weaknesses, your previous career, your future aspirations and so on. We will be exploring ways of answering these questions later.

Competency Interviews

However, the traditional interview with its style of questions isn't the only game in town, and more often today you will encounter what is usually known as a competency-based interview. Competency based interviews are predicated on the idea that how we have acted, reacted and performed in the past gives the best indication of how we will do so in future.

In order to explore this, the interviewer will be interested in, and ask you for, examples of your past performance, as well as allowing you to discuss your approach or thinking behind those actions. These are the interviews in which you will have questions such as *"Can you tell me about a time when you dealt with a difficult situation?"* or perhaps *"Can you describe a situation where your team faced the challenge of completing a project under tight time constraints, and how did you go about it?"*.

It is important with these interviews is to ensure that you have a good range of examples that show you in a favourable light, but which can also be explored in sufficient depth. There is also the need to have a wide range of carefully thought through examples to use - just going back to the same single example for every question is a mistake that can imply a lack of breadth of experience.

Behavioural Interviews

Behavioural interviews, on the other hand, are a little different. Instead of asking what you did in a past situation, they ask what you would do... They explore hypothetical scenarios, rather than actual past ones. This means that questions such as "What would you do if…." are usual here.

Preparing for the competency interview can be a good preparation for behavioural interviews too, as you can also sometimes use competency type experiences in a behavioural interview by remembering what you did (and perhaps tidying up your response depending on what you learnt from the experience) and then using it as the example of what you would do.

The answer structure to use, if you do this, is to start with what you would do, use the historical example as an illustration of this, and then refer back to the hypothetical scenario the interviewer had posed.

For instance, if you were asked what you would do if you encountered an angry customer:

"I would ensure that I really listened and understood the situation before I tried to resolve it. For example, a short while ago I had a really challenging customer who was really angry because they felt that the product they had received was faulty. I started by listening carefully to them, so that I would understand and not misinterpret the reasons for the problem, and because I felt it important that the customer did feel that their complaint had been taken seriously. Then, when I fully understood the reasons behind their anger, I discussed it with them and offered a really good solution that they were happy with. So, if that happened to me again, I would ensure that I listened and then try to find the best outcome for both the customer and the organisation…."

Strength Based Interviews

A strength-based interview will be focused more on your likes and interests. Strength based interviews assume that you will perform far better in a role that aligns with what you enjoy doing. For example, if you like being around and interacting with people, then it is likely that you would be well suited to a customer facing role.

The strengths interview is based around a positive approach, and because of this, the interviewer should explore your strengths in more depth, rather than talking about weaknesses. It will focus upon positives such as skills and experience, and also how you are developing yourself and moving forward.

Values Based Interviews

Values based interviews are predicated around whether your personal values align well with the values of the organisation. For example, one of the values of the organisation may be a focus upon the customer, and so if you are someone that enjoys working with people and has a personal focus upon the customer and the importance of delivering a good customer experience, then you are aligned, and things should go well.

It's obviously important to be aware of the values of the organisation before the interview (they are often to be found on the organisations website) and be able to put across how your own values align with them. Expect also, competency type questions based around values – for example *"Can you give is an example of when you feel you demonstrated integrity within the workplace?"*.

Technical Interviews

Focused on technical specialities, preparation will involve ensuring that you can talk about relevant experience and technical ability. An additional focus will often also be on your professional development, and how you are keeping up to date with the field.

It's important to be able to demonstrate this, and so have examples of courses or other CPD you have recently undertaken, as well as how you are applying this learning.

Informal Interviews

Some organisations also like to try an informal interview approach. This interview may be in a much more relaxed setting in the form of a free-flowing conversation, perhaps over coffee. You won't necessarily be asked questions in the same way as a formal interview, but often many of the same issues will be introduced in a much subtler way.

The interviewer will have points that they wish to explore, but if they are good at what they are doing you may not realise just how much they are probing your abilities and experience. These interviews have also been used as confirmatory events after a formal interview, introducing applicant to additional interested parties and getting their opinions.

An informal interview can help you to relax and put you at your ease, which is useful, but do be careful because it's very easy in a situation like this to be lulled into a false sense of security and relax too much, at which point things could slip out that you might later regret – don't be too candid!

Remember, this is still an interview, however easy going it might appear on the surface.

Going into informal interviews will still require all the preparation we will be discussing later such as knowing your strengths etc. You just need to work them into the conversation.

Bringing It All Together

As I mentioned at the start, many of these different interview types are quite similar at the end of the day. Really, it's all about you, what you are good at and what you aren't, the skills you bring and the experiences that you have behind you - as well as how you used or learnt from them. How the questions may be asked will vary, but the information really should not be that different.

Also, be aware that often interviews sometimes do the unexpected – especially recently - and can throw in unexpected questions. So, if they suggest that the interview will be competency based, do not be surprised if you still get strength based, traditional or technical questions as well.

So, prepare well, don't let surprises in interview phase you, and you should sail through...

Before You Apply...

Your preparation for an interview should really start before you have even begun to apply for jobs. I know that may sound excessive, but there could be some very important issues to address. We live in the age of the internet, and that means that a surprising amount of crucial information about you may be instantly available for your potential employers – all they have to do is a simple online search...

Therefore, there are a few things that you may find very helpful to do before you have sent your CV to anyone, let alone reached interview stage...

LinkedIn and other Similar Sites

If you have a LinkedIn account, make sure that it says what you want it to say to create the image that you wish to project. LinkedIn is used and consulted for many different jobs, so a presence here can be important, and it does contribute towards the impression an employer will get.

Make it professional and suited to the job that you are looking for in terms of the qualifications you put up etc. LinkedIn is a good opportunity for your potential employers to get a rounded idea about you, so it's worth crafting a good profile on the platform if you decide to use it.

Social Media.

Something that many potential employers could do, either before or after interview, is an internet and social media search for you. So, before you start applying for those wonderful new career positions, and subsequently go for the interview, what does your online and social media presence say about you?

It may seem somewhat unreasonable for potential employers to invade your privacy by looking at social media, checking up on you outside the work domain. After all, much of your online presence may well be about your own free time outside work. In addition, there are possibly issues with potential employers using 'private' information found online as part of a hiring decision.

But remember that we are talking real world here, and so issues such as privacy won't always stop people looking to make their life easier, and to make their decisions as risk averse as possible.

Consider your social media profile. Does it paint the picture of a reliable conscientious individual, who is dedicated and who will deliver outstanding results for the organisation, or do you perhaps instead come across as a drunken party animal who shouldn't be let loose near anyone or anything important?...

Unfortunately, the internet can be pretty much forever, and so those hilarious pictures that you posted for student friends to see 5 years ago of you flat on the floor in a drunken stupor could remain as an indicator of your reliability as a potential employee today. And this means pictures that are not only on your own social media accounts, but also on other peoples...

Also, how about your social media comments - not just those on your own account but again other people's accounts and social media feeds that you have commented upon? Can your comment, which at the time seemed to be humorous, on-point and perhaps a bit edgy, now be construed as racist, sexist, ageist, or anything else that might be deemed problematic? Those comments that seemed so funny to share with the world 5 years ago could now hanging over you and your path to success.
Time to do something about it and have an online spring clean...

The first thing to do is to Google yourself. By the way, don't just try Google but other search engines as well. Ensure that you find everything about you that is available online. By the way, before you do that make sure that you have signed out of Google etc, as if you are logged in the search suggestions will be personalised and won't necessarily match what others may find.

Of course, if there are skeletons in your cupboard, this could be when you are delighted if you have an extremely common name, as that will make it more difficult to find you specifically. Search under the name you have given in your CV, as well as your shortened more commonly used version. So, search under 'David' as well as 'Dave' for instance.

Once you have found all the references about you online that you can, examine them and decide if they paint the picture now that you really want others (such as your potential employers) to see. Then, you may feel it wise to try to erase elements of that old content that could scupper your application as possible. Of course, this is where you may find out just how 'sticky' the information on the internet can be – getting rid of things can be challenging.

After the general online search, make sure that you have spruced up your social media presence, as anything that might count against you could be located and so prevent you getting the job. Again, remove anything that could be misconstrued, as even with strong privacy settings it is surprising what can slip through.

Privacy settings can be interesting, and even useful. If your social media profile makes you look pretty good – lots of pictures of you volunteering and doing community projects for example, running a marathon for charity and things like that - you may want to allow some public access as it can show you in a good light. Alternatively, after reviewing the material, if there are things you cannot spring clean you may want to lock your Facebook etc privacy settings down tighter than Fort Knox…

Actually, do double check those privacy settings even if you think that they are already set to the maximum, as updates seem to reset settings such as this far too often…Also, don't forget it's not just your own pictures and posts, but those that you may be tagged in on other people's pages…

It is, of course, entirely up to you if you want to follow the advice in this section, but it could make a difference. One other obvious, yet important, point - don't try to suddenly and obviously fill your profile with pictures of you doing incredible good deeds and living a healthy productive life. It's noticeable if everything has been posted over a period of just two days, shortly before you sent in your application! Interviewers aren't stupid – they will notice…

Top Tips

- Do an online search for yourself.
- Tidy and remove anything which may count against you.
- Check those privacy settings!

Telephone and Video Interviews

With the advent of better communication and internet technology and particularly with the recent pandemic, remote interviews in the form of either telephone or video interviews have become increasingly popular.

The first key point is to treat them, at least as much as possible, as you would a face-to-face interview. However, there are some differences including some you can use to your advantage...

Using Notes

In a telephone interview, they can't see you, and in a video interview, they can't necessarily see what you can see. This means that, unlike face-to-face interviews, these interviews will give you an excellent opportunity to have some notes at the ready. This can be really useful for reminding you to say everything that you want to say and helps to prevent the mind going blank under pressure.

I would definitely recommend having *some* notes to hand. However, ideally don't use them unless you really have to, and be very aware of the temptation to try to have too many notes in front of you as this could mean not being able to find what you are looking for at crucial moments.

Instead, if you want to use notes then prepare them carefully and just have bullet points or use a mind map to lay out the main points in a logical sequence or framework. All you need is a reminder of the points you wish to cover - never a complete script.

For a telephone interview, lay it out on a maximum of a couple of pages so that you can find what you need nice and quickly, and on a video interview perhaps on notes around the screen – just make sure they won't fall off during the interview!

Think, also, about where your notes are if you have them. In in video interview, if your camera is on the top of your screen, do you want to print out your notes and BluTak them to the wall, above, as well as having things on the screen below, to stop you having to look too far away from the camera and be obviously referring to notes. If you do BluTak them, make sure they will stay up there!

With video interview notes, you really do not want it to be too obvious that you are looking at them – it looks unprofessional. However, remember that we don't tend to look at people all of the time when we are talking anyway, and we often look away to think. This means that, if the notes are placed correctly, you can make it look as if you are simply looking away for the camera to consider your answer for a moment. Hence the placing of any notes is important to make it look natural.

Top Tips

- If you are going to use notes, just use bullet points.
- Try not to use them unless absolutely necessary.
- Position any notes so you can glance at them discretely.

Telephone Interviews

During telephone interviews, your tone of voice becomes even more important, since the interviewer cannot gain additional information via body language. Thus, it will make an even larger impact on the overall impression that the interviewer forms of you - sounding confident and positive about your answers is vital.

On the telephone, also ensure that you answer the question fully, as you have no behavioural cues from the interviewer which we may use to become aware when we've said enough in a face to face interview.

By the same token, there are no cues to say you have said enough so there is a danger of rambling on. Because of this, having a really effective structure to your answer to ensure that it is full without being too verbose.

If you are using a mobile phone, bear in mind that technology can let you down. Before the call make sure, for instance, your phone is fully charged to avoid it running out of charge halfway through the interview and dying on you.

Also, ensure that you are in a place where there is a good mobile signal to avoid dropouts – check this beforehand as you don't want to be rushing around or waving your phone around frantically trying to pick up a good signal just as the interview is about to start.

If you are likely to be on your mobile in an area where coverage is sparse, do remember that certain times of day tend to get busy on the networks which means that it can be more difficult at these times to get a reliable signal.

One approach that can be useful for a telephone interview is to use a headset microphone, rather than just holding the phone to your ear. This can help to ensure that your own speech will be easy for the interviewer to hear as the microphone is in a constant position, and its far better than having the phone on speakerphone which can make the room sound echoey.

Also, having your hands free can make a difference in finding your notes, and also to me at least, makes things more relaxed and helps concentration on the conversation. Try it out, but if you do get a headset microphone test it out beforehand to make sure it works properly, and you have the microphone in the best position for clear speech.

Top Tips
- In telephone interviews, tone of voice is even more important.
- Structure your answer well.
- Consider using a headset with microphone.
- Check mobile signal and battery level before you start!

Video Interviews

Of course, video interviews using Zoom, Teams, Google or similar also are also becoming increasingly a part of the interview scene. Again, there are some issues to bear in mind with video interviews – in fact a surprising number so we'll work through the key ones.

The first consideration is whether you want to be interviewed while you are using a desktop PC or with the camera on your phone or tablet. The quality will vary depending on the technology you use. Look at your options and see which one gives you the clearest picture – a nice sharp picture helps to give the best impression. Usually, you will find that laptops and desktops are far easier to set up to give a good framing etc. than mobiles or tablets.

Crucial, and often overlooked until too late, is to make sure that you have downloaded and installed the videocall software you will need well ahead of time. The last thing you want is to be getting close to the interview time whilst desperately trying to find, download and get the program you need installed.

Make sure that you really do know how to use whatever video conferencing software you will be using... There are similarities between them, but also each definitely has its own idiosyncrasies that are well worth knowing about and mastering before the day. Waiting until your interview is imminent before you start to work out how to use the particular program they have said they will be using can be doomed to failure, or at least increased stress. The last you want to do is to feel anxious with the clock ticking down to the interview whilst you are struggling to use the program effectively…

Ensure that you log-on a little bit ahead of time to ensure that there are no connection problems.

Check that you know how to switch the video from your camera on and off, and can you unmute the microphone or adjust its level if you need to? Try it out and make sure that you do.

If you are giving a PowerPoint or similar presentation online or wish to show a document or anything else to the interviewer during the interview you need to ensure that you know how to share a screen or window within the program that you are using. If your presentation has video or audio, there are often additional checkboxes that need to be ticked when beginning sharing, so make sure you understand and can locate those.

Also, if you are trying to share a screen to show a presentation during the interview, but it isn't allowing you then don't panic – if the interviewer initiated the online meeting, they may not have enabled other people to share in the software, so you may need to request them to do this.

With online video interviews, if you don't have a high-quality internet connection try to make sure there's no one else in the house hogging the bandwidth you want to use as this can make the video stream jerky. Having a jerky image may not necessarily be terrible, and really shouldn't change impression of the interviewer on the other end, but it actually it can do so. Everything feeds into the impression that we give, consciously or subconsciously, so you want a nice clear smooth streaming video if at all possible.

Hopefully, you will be positioned with a strong signal and no-one else stealing the bandwidth, but sometimes even then gremlins can get into the technology and a connection problem can suddenly emerge. If this is the case, and the video is jerky and the connection shows no sign of improving, then sometimes switching off your video camera and just using audio will allow an unbroken conversation to resume. It isn't ideal, but if there is no alternative it may be better to request to the interviewer that you could so this than have a really broken-up video conversation.

Now make sure your technology is working properly – is your microphone working and can people hear you clearly when you speak? Is the camera good enough to provide a clear image? These can both make an impression, so test them out with a friend online to make sure that they are good enough. I've encountered far too many poor quality or malfunctioning cameras, and especially microphones, to be certain that a given unit will function correctly without checking first.

Personally, when I'm videoconferencing, I like using a desktop PC, and headphones with a headset microphone as this prevents annoying audio feedback and enables me to hear whoever I'm working with clearly, as well as making my own voice clearer for the listener.

Be aware that just using the microphone on the phone or laptop can make the sound echoey, so if you are using just this then check out how it sounds the other end. A room with a lot of soft furnishings tends to dampen the echo more than a bare room.

Top Tips

- Use a laptop/desktop rather than a phone or tablet.
- Check you have the right software installed.
- Make sure you can use the software, including switching camera on and off and muting your microphone.
- Do you need to share a screen, perhaps for a presentation? If so, make sure you know how.
- Double check your WiFi signal, and make sure no-one else is hogging your bandwidth.
- Log on early.
- Make sure your camera works well, and especially that your microphone gives a clear quality sound. Consider using a headset.

If you can, find a quiet location and, crucially, make sure you won't be disturbed - having crying child or barking dog in the background can be distracting for both you and the interviewer. Try and find somewhere quiet and private to have that interview and yes, even go as far as the make sure that the room door is shut so the cat doesn't come in and wander happily through the field of view at a critical moment!

Think about lighting. If there is a window behind you, then you'll be silhouetted and so they won't be able to see you properly. A bright light within the image can have the same effect. Another element can be time of day - if you are being interviewed in the afternoon, depending on the time of year, it may begin to get dark, and so what started as a well-lit view of you using natural light can find you gradually disappearing into the gloom of twilight. I've been on a few videocalls, where the person the other end has been invisible by the time we had finished our conversation!

Also be aware that the background behind you is clean and tidy, rather than looking cluttered and chaotic. All these things will form an impression in the minds of the interviewer the other end of the video link.

With a webcam, and even more so if using your phone or tablet, think about how you are going to set it up to look at you. Quite often using a phone or tablet camera in a way which is comfortable for you can end up giving some very strange camera angles for the person the other end! A camera angle of looking straight up your nose really isn't great for the interviewer…

This isn't usually the case when sitting at the PC with an attached or integrated WebCam but you still want to think about its placing as you need to be able to look into the camera as much as possible to create 'eye contact' with the interviewer. Do remember to do this – because we naturally often focus upon the window on the screen where the other person appears, rather than the camera, our eyeline is such that we aren't seeming to look at the interviewer properly. To remedy this, make sure you do at least sometime look at the camera, especially when they are talking to you or asking a question.

Have a look and think about the framing of the image that the interviewer will see, such as how far away you are from the camera you are. Does your face feel the field of view or are you a tiny dot in the distance? Actually, somewhere in between is usually best as if your face is totally filling the screen, it can actually be a little bit disconcerting for the person the other end, whilst being too distant can give the feeling of disconnection!

Also, a better framing gives you a bit more chance for elements of your positive body language to show through as well.

Online video interviews are fairly new, and if you are unused to talking in a video call, I would suggest it is well worth some practice to become more familiar with the concept. At first some people find it unnerving, although with familiarity you can actually forget that you are talking through a computer. Set up a couple of calls with friends to get used to talking online and seeing people via the screen.

Dress as if you were going to a face-to-face interview. Don't let the virtual nature of the interview allow you to feel you can get away with being more casually dressed. Dress to impress!

It's very easy to ignore body language in a video interview, but it still has an important place. A good upright posture, engagement through eye contact with the camera, and passion for the position can be backed up by use of the hands – just be aware of the camera framing and check that your hands can be seen!

Top Tips

- Think of location, lighting, background, and framing.
- Think of the camera angle.
- Dress as for a face-to-face interview
- Use your body language.
- Practice!

Research

If you want to be confident, then you need to go into the interview as fully prepared as possible - and that means some research.

One of the most common interview mistakes is not knowing nearly enough about the organisation that they are applying to, or the role that they are applying for within it. I have seen people seriously flounder in their interview because of this. A little research can make a considerable difference to performance in interview, not just because of any questions that may come up, but also for building your inner confidence for the interview as walking into an organisation applying for a role that you know a lot about can help boost your confidence.

Some questions to think about:
1. Who are they really looking for? - what skills and mindset will the successful applicant need?
2. What does the position really involve?
3. What is the organisation like?
4. What is the organisations ethos and how is it developing?

Answering these questions can help you to prepare.

Now, you may be arranging several interviews, and so may feel that you don't have time to really research each one in depth. However, each interviewer will want to feel that you are passionate about their organisation – and their organisation above all others.

They should be made to feel that, even if they know that you are going for other interviews, this is the interview you have been saving yourself for, and there is there is nowhere else that you would really want to work. Research helps to make this happen. If time is really precious, focus your research upon the role you feel best about.

Research is key and a great time investment. Let us explore that a little…

Researching the organisation

First port of call is to take a look at the organisation's website. Get a feel for them - is it a small organisation or a large one? Does it have its fingers in many different business pies, or is it a specialist organisation that just focuses on one area? What part of the organisation are you trying to join, and what can you find out about it?

One of the key points that you need to clarify for yourself here is why is this firm particularly interesting to you, and why do you want to work there? This can be a question that interviewers ask, so having a clear answer is important.

Top Tip
- Get a good feel for the organisation.
- Make sure that you have a clear idea why you want to work for that organisation.

On the website look the things that give you a clue to the philosophy and approach of the organisation. Is it a very laid-back employee-centred organisation or is it very focused on simply business and making money? Do you feel that they pride themselves in the way they look after people or are you there simply to provide something for them?

The mission statement or similar of the values of the organisation can be quite important here and it can be really useful to be able to quote this in the interview. By the way if you do so, don't be surprised if the panel themselves quite don't know their own mission statement – although that itself will tell you something about the organisation!

Check whether there are organisational news pages on the site about what's going on there or even blogs from people within it? All these things will give you a goodfeel for them and where they are going.

Also being able to bring this out in the interview it can raise you above other applicants. Crucially you may want to find out one or two pieces of news that you can use later on in the interview itself to show your understanding of the organisation. Perhaps they are due to open new manufacturing unit, or expand into new market, or there may be new legislation which is going to affect the organisation in some way. Make a note of a couple of points that you could bring out in the interview to show that you know about the organisation and are really keen to work there.

For example:

> "I understand that you have just won the national award for customer care, which is fantastic. I believe that it is really important, and so high-quality customer care is something which I feel is central to the way in which I work."

Top Tips
- Research any news about the organisation.
- What does it actually do?
- What are its values or mission statement etc?

There is additional research that you could undertake which could take it to another level if you want to. This is more time-consuming approach, but can work nicely in some situations, especially for more senior roles. For many positions such as, for example, within local authorities or the health service, it can be really impressive to find out about other similar organisations and what they are doing to give you some ideas that you can put across in the interview. This can give the impression that your finger really is on the pulse of your profession.

It can also be useful to have news from the field they operate in - what's happening in planning law, for instance, if that is relevant to the position.

This won't work at all interviews, but for many positions it can be very effective, and this is probably best illustrated by giving an example. Let's suppose you are going for a position with a local authority in their leisure and parks department. Research you conduct before the interview has indicated that another council has a new policy in their parks that has increased community usage in ways which could be relevant to the role you are applying for. That is great - let's imagine using this in the interview, when you might get a chance to bring out something like:

> *"Actually, I understand that Coventry Council have introduced a new policy of opening the parks earlier in the morning, and that has increased use by the community by over 20%. I think that that is a really interesting idea for reconnecting people to their local open spaces".*

Doesn't that sound great? Doesn't that just tell the interviewer that Parks and Leisure are something you are passionate about, and that you are aware and interested in what is happening in the wider field?

If the interviewer has heard of whatever you are using, you need to know it and understand it in enough depth to hold your own if they decide to discuss it, but if you do so, you can really create an excellent positive impression.

They may come back with related information that you are unaware of, and I'd deal with that carefully - if you start improvising too much and making things up you will be caught out. So, let's suppose that the interviewer follows your insightful comment about Coventry with something like:

> "That's really interesting. Plymouth Council are extending their opening hours too.".

You could reply

> "I hadn't seen that, but I think that it shows the possibilities of exploring that idea."

It's OK to admit that you haven't heard of something here. You have already demonstrated interest and knowledge of the field, but no-one can know everything.

Top Tip
- Try to find out ideas that are happening in similar organisations, or elsewhere in their field.

Visiting Them

There are many ways you can think of as preparation as being an investment in interview success. If it is an important interview, and most interviews are, an investment of time that many people don't utilise is to request to actually visit the organisation. If you are accepted for interview and it seems practical for the position, then why not contact them and ask them if you can pop in and find out more about the position?

Now, at the end of the day they may say 'yes' or 'no', but it really doesn't matter. If they decline your request, it still looks good because you have at least shown a willingness and an interest in the position in a way that most other applicants probably won't have.

And, if you are allowed to visit the organisation, it creates a huge opportunity. You will meet people who can give you some inside information about the organisation and role you wouldn't get from the website or external sources. When you visit you can get a feel for the type of person that is currently doing the job, and how they do it. What skills are they using? This information can be invaluable in shaping your answer in terms of your strengths and skills, and your stating of work ethic. You will also find out about the duties that the role has and be able to prepare based upon this.

Intriguingly, it can also give you information in another way. People are so focused upon putting forward what they feel the interviewers are looking for, that they miss a trick in the other direction. If you get a chance to visit and really find out about the position, you might occasionally be able to subtly get a feel of who they don't want.

What do I mean by this? Well, let's suppose you pick up during your visit that the previous occupant of the position tended to be a strictly 9 to 5, jobsworth individual, whilst the management were looking for more commitment and flexibility. This gives you the chance to put forward your flexibility and work ethic at interview increasing your match to what they are looking for. Or perhaps you may gather that they perhaps made mistakes that caused other team members problems, and so you can really stress at interview the importance of accuracy in your work. Now it doesn't necessarily happen often, but when it does it can provide you with unique information that will give you an edge, and that is worthwhile.

But there's yet another deeper reason why this visiting can be important. We are human beings and although interviews are meant to be completely unbiased and without human emotions making a difference, in fact they do. By visiting the organisation not only will you get information, but your face may also get recognised at interview. You may even talk to people on your visit who could be interviewing you on the day. You therefore could get a chance to make that first impression in a very natural much less pressured way than during the interview itself. People also prefer the familiar, which you have now just become by meeting them, and this can give you a powerful head start.

Top Tip
- Try to visit the organisation to find out more about the role.
- If you visit, try to discretely find out about the previous role holder.

On Interview Day

On interview day you will probably be nervous, and naturally when we are nervous it's easy to forget things. So, if there is anything that you need to take with you to the interview, make sure that you have made a checklist ahead of time. Perhaps a copy of your CV if needed, and even more important, the materials for your presentation if you must give one – have you got that laptop or USB stick with you? (and have you got a back-up stick just in case?...).

Now, the following is really obvious, and so you may wonder why I mention it. The reason is simply that, while I have been interviewing, I have encountered too many people who really don't seem to have realised it!

As I mention elsewhere, first impressions count, and they count in a big way. Human beings still have many very ancient and primitive responses, and our sense of smell is one of these. It remains a powerful factor in forming impressions, which is why personal freshness is so important. Make sure that you have showered and are clean and tidy as body odour is an almost instant black mark against you.

By the way, in the same vein, don't wear too much perfume or aftershave - it can be overpowering.

If you can, try not to smoke just before the interview, as that will taint your breath and stick to your clothes (smokers may not realise just how easy it is for non-smokers to detect the smell of stale smoke, and how strong and unpleasant it can be for non-smokers).

Having a mint just beforehand or chewing gum before an interview can freshen the breath. However, don't walk into the interview venue, or sit waiting, whilst chewing gum.

Dress Code

The way you actually dress at interview will also have a powerful effect upon the impression that the interviewers form about you. It is usually the first thing that they see, and so contributes to that crucial first impression. Although as we've said before an interview is meant to be completely impartial, human nature once again means that first impressions can sway things for or against you.

So, take your time to think about the right dress code for the interview. It's got a very obviously appropriate for the organisation. Once again, in my time conducting interviews I have seen all sorts of appropriate and inappropriate dress, including seeing people turning up to interviews in torn jeans etc. Believe me, that would make an impression, but probably not the one you want.

In terms of dress code, the general rule is to dress up rather than dress down, so if you are uncertain then smart and professional will probably be the way to go. Dressing casually could be appropriate for some organisations but is high-risk if you get it wrong. The peripherals are important too – make sure that shoes are shined etc. Its old fashioned, I know, but does make a difference.

I'd also suggest that high necked attire can be important as, when under pressure, people tend to flush red. This isn't great at the best of times as it shows the pressure the person feels that they are under, but chest flushing can be mostly hidden with a high-necked attire. However, where clothing is low cut, that flush can become visible creeping upward, and will clearly highlight to the panel that you are not as cool and composed as you may be trying to portray!

As well as being showered and fresh, please do ensure that your clothes are clean and fresh too. Don't go into the interview wearing yesterday's outfit, as smelling musty is not a great way of creating a positive impression. Often the interview will be in a small room, perhaps on a hot day, and so a sweaty shirt is not great... Indeed, if it is a hot day, and indeed even if it isn't, although that isn't often practical, if you are able to change into your interview clothes and freshen up shortly before the interview it can make a pleasant difference.

Top Tips
- Ensure you are fresh, clean and tidy
- Dress code is important - dress up not down.
- High necked attire can hide nervous flushing...

The Journey

Make sure that you know exactly where the interview is – because we can sometimes be surprised as organisations buildings can be harder to find than we expect. If you aren't local to the interview and so checking beforehand is difficult, use Google Street view to get the feel for the location and where the interview itself will take place so you can find it easily and without getting flustered by running late.

Leave plenty of time to get there, but not so much that you will be waiting around for too long. Get to the location, and perhaps go and look around somewhere if you are early. This can help to avoid being stressed during the interview, which can of course happen if you are running late and can throw off your whole interview game if you are not careful. It's well worth avoiding by being careful about time.

Sometimes, the unavoidable happens and you cannot arrive on time. A major road accident, train line stoppage, or whatever can make a difference. If so, contact the organisation at the first safe opportunity (not from your moving car whilst you are driving) and explain the situation to them. They may be able to juggle their schedule, but at the very least they will now why you are late and that it isn't your fault.

They may still interview you on the same day, and if so, don't let being late fluster you – think of it that you have been given a completely new time for your interview rather than being late for the original one.

Don't drink too much coffee as that can make you jittery, and alcohol is right out – the smell of booze on your breath is an instant fail. Indeed, don't generally drink too much of anything beforehand as being desperate to use the toilet isn't great for your concentration and focus.

Top Tips
- Check location beforehand – Google Streetview can be useful here.
- Give yourself plenty of time - don't arrive late and flustered.
- Don't drink too much before the interview.

Arriving

Before you walk in, it's vital to switch off your mobile phone to ensure that it will not ring with a caller or chime as it receives messages during the interview.

Do remember that every single contact you have with the organization can count – even reception etc may well be asked to give their option about you and how you conduct yourself. Many years ago, I remember interviewing a lady who happily told us how she was diplomatic and excellent at dealing with people. After her interview, our receptionist vented loudly about how rude the lady had been to her when she had arrived. This didn't help her case, so be pleasant and polite to everyone...

Waiting

While you are sitting there, it's best not to play with your phone. It can be very tempting to do so, as it distracts us and helps us to keep calm, but it can look unprofessional and as if you have a short attention span.

Sit calmly, running through the interview in your mind and relaxing and centring yourself as much as possible, perhaps using the techniques that we examine elsewhere. You will be nervous – of course you will – but this can add to your interview performance rather than taking it away as long as the interview anxiety isn't too overwhelming. Remember, we explore tips and tools for improving interview confidence and reducing anxiety in other sections.

Top Tips
- Turn your mobile to silent before entering the venue.
- Every contact counts - give a great impression!
- While waiting, calm and centre yourself - don't play with your phone.

Creating a Great First Impression

Now let's have a think about that crucial moment when you first step into the interview room itself, seeing the interviewers waiting for you.

This can be a nerve-wracking moment - what happens in the next few minutes could bring you large financial improvement, new job security, interesting work days, fascinating new people to meet, and generally could change your life… So, no pressure then…

Of course, you are likely to be nervous, so remember that if you have butterflies as you are going into your interview then it is highly likely that everyone else going in to interview will have them too.

Now you might be reassured by the idea that the people interviewing you are professionals who will leave their own feelings, opinions and biases outside the room, with the outcome will be purely decided by the objective quality of your answers. However, in reality the people sitting on the other side of the desk are human beings, subject to the same human biases as everyone else. This is important because, for example, if an interviewer is scoring an applicants answer and is uncertain of what score to give, but they like the interviewee as a person, there will be a tendency to give them the benefit of the doubt and round their score up - not consciously or deliberately, but because human nature subtly influences what we actually do.

Therefore, if they dislike the applicant, they could be subconsciously more critical and mark them down for the same given answer - and this can make a difference. It's important to reiterate here that the interviewer won't normally do this deliberately, or even be aware of it, but instead it can occur subconsciously.

So, we need to use human biases to our advantage as much as we can, so let's try to think about what can swing things in your favour.

Firstly – we need to impress, and the key here is the importance of those first impressions, as we form opinions of people the moment we see them. Various figures are often quoted as to how long it takes for us to form our initial impression about someone, with somewhere about 7 seconds being popular. However long it is (and it will vary between individual interviewers) it certainly is close enough to instantly. Now that first impression is important, as we will tend to view everything else in relation to this first perception which can be hard to change – not impossible, but certainly challenging..

The factors that create this initial impression include body language, our appearance, dress and our initial greeting to the interviewer. Taking these in likely order of impression formation…

We have already talked about dress in the section about preparation, so won't repeat it here. However, I would ensure before you enter the building, and again before the interview that you check your clothing to make sure that it is neat and not askew and that I does not look like you just dragged yourself out of bed having slept overnight in your clothes!

We are going to explore more details about body language elsewhere, but remember that the next element that can create an impression is your smile. A smile is an ancient body language gesture, which shows confidence and can begin to build rapport. Do smile, as you walk in and see the interviewers for the first time.

Secondly, in interviews – confidence sells. You need to look confident as you walk in, and the key to this is that smile, but combined with an upright posture and good eye contact with members of the panel. This can make a great first impression, as well as help you to start to overcome your nerves as it is believed that our posture can influence how we feel.

Handshakes?... Well, the jury is still out on handshakes, and whether they are a good thing. As a general principle, I believe that generally (pandemics excluded), they are, as they can convey both professionalism and a level of confidence and assurance that you wish to project. If you do decide to shake hands, then make it a positive handshake but don't overdo it - in my time interviewing I have encountered everything from the limp lettuce handshake (damp and floppy – not good) to the bone crusher (I seem to remember feeling my knuckles actually grinding against each other - also not ideal...). In this latter case the individual took the usual advice to have a firm handshake a little too far!

Now, introduce yourself to the panel - ideally thanking the panel for seeing you.

"Good morning, I'm Andrea Trent. Thank you for seeing me today."

is a powerful and polite start to the interview, and again shows that you are feeling confident and positive.

Even better could be:

"Good morning, I'm Andrew Trent. Thank you for seeing me today. I'm looking forward to sharing with you what I feel I could bring to the organisation."

Your voice should be professional and calm or positive and enthusiastic. Beware of a monotone, or the shaky voice caused by nerves. We will talk in more detail about using your voice later.

Top Tips

- The first 7 seconds you encounter the interviewer creates a key impression about you.
- Dress code is important.
- Smile, and have an upright, confident posture.
- Deliver a positive greeting.

About Your Interviewers

When they go into an interview, many people tend to feel that the panel are trying to trip them up or catch them out. That is not the case, and in fact, just the opposite is usually happening, as most interviewers really want you to do well.

The panel may look stern, but in my experience of working with interview panels this may not be for the reasons you assume. You see, your interviewers may be less used to interviewing than you think, and so any stern face and lack of visible emotion may be down to them either trying too hard to be 'professional' and fair to all applicants, and/or because they actually are nervous themselves. Yes, it's true. Your interview panel can be as nervous as you are! Many people don't enjoy sitting in judgement of others.

Therefore, putting the panel at its ease is as important as many other elements. Smile, be human. Thank them for seeing you. Those first few seconds are important, and if in those first few seconds the panel feel that you are someone they will enjoy talking to, then you are off to a flying start.

Top Tips
- Remember, your interviewer really wants you to do well.
- Don't assume a stern countenance from your interviewer is negative - they may be nervous about interviewing!

Interview Answers - An Introduction

Now of course, it would be natural to assume that in interviews there would be an almost limitless variety of possible questions that could be asked, and if that was the case, it could make preparation somewhat challenging.

Don't worry though because it's not as bad as it may seem. Although the actual content and structure of the individual questions can vary greatly, there are still only a few topics that most interviewers will want to know about. This means if you think about and prepare these topic areas, rather than simply finding scripted answers to very specific questions, you will be much better prepared. During coming sections, we will be doing just that.

Rehearsing Your Answers

Remember, the questions we explore may not be asked these in exactly the wordings suggested, but the underlying intent will be there. Rehearse how you are going to answer them. It is worth rehearsing your answers several times to hone them until they flow naturally and easily.

A great idea that can be very effective is to actually record your answers to the questions, perhaps on your mobile phone, and then play them back to yourself. Record several questions and your answers, and then leave it for an hour or more (or even next day) so that you hear them back fresh. They always sound differently when you are listening to them this way, just as the interviewer would hear them, and it enables you to think about your answers more dispassionately and critically. Although many people really hate hearing themselves recorded, it's only you going to be you that is listening, and it will give you a chance to really reflect and improve those answers!

If you do this, do be really critical of your answers, and redo them until they sound right to you. Doing this is no substitute for an experienced professional interview coach, but it certainly better than not reflecting on your answers.

Top Tip
- Rehearse your answers - record them and play them back after a time gap to hear how they sound.

Now it is important to practice your answers but try not to memorise the exact words for two important reasons. Firstly, this can sound artificial and over-rehearsed, making it sound as it you are reading from a script.

Secondly, the question may be somewhat different to the one that you have actually rehearsed, and so it can then be challenging to change your answer to answer the actual one posed, rather than the question you were expecting. It doesn't look good if you adopt the politicians approach of answering the question you wanted to answer, rather than the actual one you were asked

Top Tip
- Practice, but be aware that memorising verbatim answers has pitfalls.

Using Notes in a Face-to-Face Interview

One of the most common questions that I am asked is whether it is acceptable to take notes into an interview. In terms of the sense that most people mean it, which is to have notes about answers to questions, the answer is unfortunately usually 'no' as interview panels will usually take a dim view of this.

It is often acceptable to have a notebook or pad with questions you may want to ask the interviewers at the end of the interview. However even here, not using notes will give a better impression.

When it comes to telephone and video interviews, the situation is potentially different - find out more in the telephone and video interview section.

Who Are They Looking For?

Before you start practicing how you are going to answer interview questions you need to decide what information you will need to have at your fingertips to answer them well. Your answers really need to fill in the blanks of what they are looking for. So naturally the first port of call is the job description or person specification.

You will need to think about the skills, experience, and type of person that they are looking for. Start with educational and job-related qualifications, and then your work experience. Then think about how these relate to the position, and what evidence you can use to support your answers that fits with it.

Using Your History

The next element to think about are your experiences that you can use as examples in the interview, especially for competency interviews. You will need a range of these, so let's pick some out and work our way through a few of the possibilities.

Depending on the role you are going for – you are much less likely to be asked for examples of your leadership if this is your first job, for example - you usually need a couple of examples of each of the following topic areas that are relevant to the position:

- Demonstrating Leadership
- Building Relationships
- Dealing with Conflict
- Overcoming Obstacles
- Finding Novel Solutions
- Your Greatest Achievements
- Integrity and Professionalism
- Making Decisions
- Dealing with Deadlines/Time Management
- Changing your Mind/Learning from Failure

Top Tip
- Ensure that you have great examples ready for competency type questions.

Think about the types of examples you may need - communication is pretty universal for instance.

Modesty and Answers

One of the biggest challenges of answering interview questions effectively is often natural modesty and not wanting to appear big-headed. Because of this we don't emphasise or push our strengths forward enough.

The interview is certainly a place where you should put our modesty aside – don't be too over the top but confidence and self-assurance about ourselves, our skills and our experience, sells in an interview.

Top Tip
- Don't go over the top, but don't be too modest in an interview - sell yourself...

Just Answer the Question!

There are a few important and universal principles to bear in mind when it comes to answering questions. Firstly - and crucially - have you actually answered the question?

It is so easy for us, especially when we are under pressure, to not really listen to the question. Thus, we answer what we think the interviewer has said and not what they really asked, or more often, give the answer that we have prepared which was actually prepared for a subtly different question (this is one of the reasons for not being too scripted in your preparation).

Allied with this is whether you have answered ALL of the question. This is crucial on multipart questions, where I have often seen people answering the main part of a question but miss out the supplementary part. In three-part questions, it tends to be the first and third part of the answer that is answered and the middle element missed out...

Listen, and ensure you answer all the question. If you are able, jot down a few key words from the question to keep you on track.

Top Tip
- Ensure you answer the question actually asked - listen!
- Ensure you answer all parts of a multipart question.

Starting and Finishing Your Answer

One of the most common questions I get asked is how to start an answer to the question. Naturally, it will very much depend on the question, but as a general approach, if you can't think of a good way to start your answer, use the keywords from the question itself. So, if you have been asked for an example of when you communicated effectively, you might start with:

"I think that a good example of my using effective communication is…"

It's simple, and helps you focus the answer upon what has been asked.

To finish an answer, one way is to again use the question:

"… and I feel that was an excellent example of effective communication".

which brings your answer to a natural conclusion.

Interview Questions – When Things Go Wrong

Now, if only every interview we attended went perfectly, things would be so easy. But of course, that is not the case. We are fallible human beings living in an imperfect world, and the upshot of this is that things can easily go wrong in your interview.

In fact, I think we can easily go further and say that almost certainly something WILL go wrong in your interview. That is the way that things work. You are under pressure, so it's little wonder that some things will go a bit awry – you may mishear a question, or may forget an important element of your answer, or perhaps you may fall into one of the traps we will explore, such as telling a rambling story about your experiences rather than a well-focused answer.

So, the best approach is to acknowledge that this will probably happen to you, and work with that fact rather than letting a mistake throw your whole interview. And don't forget, your competition - those other applicants who are also being interviewed – certainly won't have a perfect interview either.

Just as we assume that all the other applicants will be calm and confident when they almost certainly are not, we also incorrectly assume they will give a perfect interview, which is again highly unlikely. You are therefore not alone!

Let's explore the different things that can crop up in the interview and take a look at some ways of dealing with them.

Forgetting the Question

Possibly the most common interview mistake – one that I've seen people make countless times - is when we realise that we have actually forgotten the question that the interviewer has just asked us! In the pressure of the interview our mind can go blank and the actual question slips from our mind. There is little you can do here but to ask them to repeat the question - simply trying to guess what they said is obviously likely to lead to disaster.

Remember, they will know that you are nervous and that our minds play tricks, including going blank, so it's often not as much of a problem as you may think. It's certainly not ideal, but you can probably get away with this for one or possibly two questions but do try not to do it too often!

"I'm really sorry, but could you repeat the question please?"

Interestingly, the way that individuals deal with this seems to vary depending on the level of the interview. Most people try to remember the question, but applicants for very senior positions will often spend a few moments jotting down the question and thinking about it before they begin to answer. If you are able to discretely and subtly jot down one or two key words – easier in an online interview – that can help you keep your answer focused by sometimes referring back to it.

Wandering Off the Question

Another common error in interviews is to start answering the actual question, but then find you are wandering away from it down some conversational cul-de-sac... There are two ways to deal with this when you realise that this is what has happened – firstly to try to guide the answer back to the actual question itself. This can actually be more challenging than it sounds, and can involve a lot more irrelevant talking that won't go down well with the interviewers.

However, I think that it can sometimes be quite powerful to actually admit that you are going wrong, and then refocus your answer. For example:

> *"I've realised that I may have moved away from where I wanted to go with my answer to your question. Let me refocus what I'm saying..."*

Missing Bits Out

Sometimes when we have rehearsed a great answer, or we have to do a presentation as part of the interview, we realise that we have missed something out. It might be a point that we wanted to make, or an interesting fact, or something that we have done in the past that we wanted to use as evidence of our experience. The temptation is to quickly jam whatever we have missed out back into our answer.

This can sound really disjointed, so think for a moment whether it is necessary to add it back in? Remember, only you know what you meant to say — the interviewer doesn't know anything is missing. Will it be better to add it in or just leave it? If it's vital, find a way to bring it in subtly if you can - perhaps add it to a later answer.

There are times, however when the most important thing is to say that you forgot to mention something earlier and you would like to add it now. Perhaps an approach such as:

"Whilst I'm discussing my career in sales, I'd actually like to add something to one of my earlier answers. When I worked at…"

Please be aware that sometimes interviewers will add this to your previous answer, but occasionally they won't. That's just how it goes, alas.

Top Tips

- If you can't remember it, do ask them to repeat the question.
- Try not to do this too often!
- If you wander off the point, admit it and refocus your answer.
- If you realise you missed something crucial in an earlier answer, mention it.

It's All About Me

There are a couple of important pitfalls to avoid when answering interview questions. It's important to be aware of them, as they can substantially make a difference to the impression that you create in the interview.

A common pitfall is what I call the 'all about me' syndrome. This is subtle, but important, and is where the interviewee focusses their answers exclusively around them and what's in it for them. Remember, the interviewer may not be as interested in you and what's in it for you, as about what you will be bringing to them. They will want to know that you want to contribute and move the organisation forward, not just benefit yourself.

This can come out is questions such as 'why do you want this position?' What about this answer?

"I really want to have a career which is exciting. I think that I would really enjoy the position and it would enable me to work my way up to a senior position..."

Well, in many ways it's a good answer, and does address the question. However, it's very much self-centred and focused on what in it for you. Naturally, in an interview, you need to push yourself forward, but it can be useful to put more balance, and add what you'll bring to them...

"I'm excited by the possibilities that this position offers to really contribute to the successful projects that the organisation is working on. I think that my skills would align with the role really well, so it would not only be a really exciting and engaging role for me, but also one where I could contribute in a meaningful way..."

If you were interviewing, which would sound best to you?

Now you can get away with a self-centred answer but widening that focus to a win-win for you and them can be a much more solid and persuasive way to go.

Top Tip
- Think about what is important for the organisation, not just you.

I, Not We

OK, so being too individual and self-centred isn't good, but there are times when the opposite is also true. Being part of a team is crucial in most organisations, and you will usually want to make sure that the interviewer knows you are a team player. However, there are also other times when you might find it useful to focus more on the 'I' than the 'we'.

For instance, if the interviewer asks you about a decision you have made, and you spend the answer focussing on the way 'we' made the decision, it can easily sound as if it wasn't you that actually made it, but it was instead a group process. The interviewer wants to know <u>you</u> can make effective decisions, and here you are implying that everyone else may have helped you to make the decision instead. It may seem a minor point but can make quite a difference to how your answer goes across, and I've known interviews where too much 'we' counted against the applicant.

The thing to keep in mind here is whether the answer is about what YOU as an individual did, or whether they really want to know about the team around you…

Top Tip
- Team thinking is important but remember that interviewers want to know what you did, so use the term 'I'.

Interview Questions

Question – "Tell Me Something About Yourself".

One of the most popular ways of opening the interview is for the interviewer to ask the question 'tell me something about yourself'.

This question terrifies many people, as they don't know how to approach it in a way that creates a good impression. Its difficulty might be thought surprising, after all, we know more about ourselves than anyone else. The challenge, therefore, is not about whether we know the information about ourselves - of course we do - but instead knowing just what aspects they might be looking for, and so form a focused and effective answer. Should you talk just about our career, or about us as a person outside work? What about our personality? How about our ambitions?

To start with, let's consider why this question is asked - and it is usually asked for a couple of reasons. Firstly, the interviewer will see it as a less threatening and more informal opening to the interview – one which will relax you. It may indeed do so, but as previously mentioned many people find that it does the exact opposite!

It also allows the interviewers want to get a general feel for you, and your background. They want to get a wider picture of you as an individual than that which is generated by your CV – most usually in terms of a broader view of your career, but very occasionally who you are outside work too.

This is a key part of the early impression that the interviewer gains of you. It will not be the very first impression, of course, which is gained through dress and body language etc., but as the first actual interview question often asked it will strongly add to those initial impressions. As a question designed to relax you into the interview, it is often not a scored element, but even so, it can be important in terms of building a positive impression of you, and as a frame for your other answers.

This is a classic opening question, so keep your answer focussed, and ensure that it complements the job on offer. Really, this is a chance to spend perhaps a minute or so explaining exactly why your career to date and your passion makes you ideal for the position. Remember that they have your CV, so simply restating your CV or Resume isn't going to impress. They are looking for something more – a flavour of you and who you are...

So, you need to excite the interviewer about your skills and experience that you are bringing, but also ensure that what you say is framed around the requirements of the job role you are going for.

Top Tips
- Don't let the question throw you - it's often designed to simply settle you into the interview.
- Think about framing your answer around aspects the complement the position you are applying for.

There is a timeline structure that will often work well for your answer, which is Present - Past - Future - Plus. We'll talk about the 'Plus' shortly but let's examine the first three elements first. So, you start off with an outline of your current position and role. If you have had a positive outcome or achievement in that role which is recent and relevant this is a great time to mention it.

Then it's the past – explaining your career path that took you to your current position. This should be concise and relevant – remember that they have your CV and it's easy to make this a simple recitation of that which won't engage the interviewer.

Finally, it's your aspiration and vision for your future, which naturally aligns beautifully with the position that you are going for. This, of course, if where your prior research about the company and the position that they are offering starts to really pay off!

With all these time-based elements, emphasising those aspects of experience etc. that align with the position is obviously important.

The 'Plus' is an optional element, and it's a little flavour of you outside work. Family, interests, and similar.

Top Tips
- Past - Present - Future is a good structure.
- You might also consider 'plus' - interests and you outside work.

Now ideally this should be delivered with excitement and passion, with each element smoothly segueing into the next. A really dry delivery will lose the interviewers interest and doing so right at the start of the interview really isn't an ideal way to go! Naturally, the elements to include should the positive ones – obviously don't throw in negatives here such as why you were fired from your previous position!

> *"Currently, I'm a senior buyer for Smith Inc. I've worked there in various roles for about 5 years, progressing from apprentice buyer up to senior buyer and currently handling contracts valued at over 30 million pounds. (Present).*
>
> *Prior to this, I have worked extensively within retail sales which I really enjoyed, and which taught me a lot about how to deal with challenging people – you meet people at their best and their worst in that environment and I developed many skills for dealing effectively with them! (Past).*

Now, I'm really looking to develop my career, and so when I saw this opening at Jones Inc. I was very interested as I'm aware that you are leaders in your sector. I really feel that this was somewhere that I can both further develop my career, and really make a difference to your organisation. (Future)

Outside of work, I love playing and watching football and keeping fit. (Plus)"

If you are uncertain about what they are looking for, keep your answer focused on you in the work context. Only if you feel certain, bring in a little bit from outside the world of work such as hobbies and about your personality (the positive aspects!) to add some colour and additional interest to your answer. This is best where they will illuminate and expand upon your suitability for the job – if your interests and passions align with the role then it can be powerful.

It is important to avoid anything that might be contentious and concern the panel, so avoid especially discussion of your religion or politics (unless the role involves religion or politics...). Crucially, don't ramble on and on with this answer – keep it concise, relevant, and interesting. Perhaps a minute or so, although this will depend on the type of interview. Remember a minute is about 100 to 130 words or so...

So, what are we looking at for preparation? Think about the organisation and the position you are going for and shape your answer around this. Include specific markers and metrics of your previous successes (for instance, doubling sales).

Whether to add in the 'Plus' element, such as more personal details such as interests and hobbies is always a challenging point. Overall, I feel that it often isn't a bad thing as it can add a little more flavour but be aware of what you are saying and only do so briefly. Your answer shouldn't become a detailed explanation of the joys of clog dancing, even if that is your thing! Of course, if you do charity or voluntary work, this can be a good time to mention this to boost your socially minded credentials.

> *"Currently, I am working within the textile industry, developing new markets for high-quality fabrics, and I feel that I've been successful there, doubling the company's sales within key emerging markets. Before that, I worked in marketing in two other sectors, aviation and computers, and it was there that I realised that marketing is where my passions and skills really lie. I'm someone who enjoys new challenges which is why I'm really excited about the position you are offering at your organisation. It's something where, moving forwards, I feel I could use my communication and marketing skills to the fullest here, as I've got a passion for developing new sales markets. Outside of work, I'm a competitive runner, and I'm aiming to improve my time in the next London Marathon where I'm running for Cancer Research. "*

Top Tips

- If you do add in about outside work, keep it positive - charity work is great!
- Avoid contentious topics - religion or politics - where possible.

Question – "Tell Me Something That's Not On Your CV"

This is a less common interview question but does come along occasionally. It is quite a quirky question and provides a great opportunity to broaden the interviewers appreciation of you, your personality and your drive. It can be used either as an early and more informal question to help you relax and open up, and to break out of the usual interview mode, or alternatively as a probing question to find out about you more deeply.

The challenge is often to know whether to talk more deeply about an aspect of your career which can demonstrate ability but be quite dry or tell them something about yourself outside work - maybe something quirky or humorous to demonstrate personality.

The best suggestion here is to get a feel for the panel, in the way that they ask it. Are they looking for that personality quirk - something interesting about you - or are they seriously set on you in the workplace?

If you are unsure, sometimes a combination of both will create a good answer. It's also worth thinking about an answer for both routes.

So, if they are looking for something about you in the workplace, you can still add an interesting element or anecdote. For instance, sharing a positive facet that won't be on your CV such as your own work ethic, and an outcome from it:

"I always like to go the extra mile when completing a project. At my last organisation, I was so focused upon getting a vital element of a project completed that I lost track of time and got locked in the office!"

Secondly, you could try sharing more of the personal you, but aspects of you that relate or resonate with the position on offer...

> *"Well, that's an interesting question. One thing that isn't on my CV is that I'm a championship ballroom dancer. I love the challenge of competition and winning, but also its fascinating putting together the steps and being aware of all the other couples on the dancefloor and adjusting and moving around them..."*

Whichever route you decide to go down, ensure that whatever you talk about is positive. No moaning or negativity here!

Top Tip
- Think about an aspect of your career, work approach, or experience, as well as a surprising or interesting element of yourself outside work.

Question – "Why do you want to work for this organisation?"

An alternate version of this question is *'Why do you want this position'*, and whichever version you encounter it is a simple question, although often one found challenging to construct a good answer for. This is because, sometimes the truthful answer is simply 'to pay the mortgage' – not what the panel will be looking for! The interviewer will want you to be keen to work for their organisation particularly, which means even if they know you have gone for other interviews, you want to put across that this is the one you really want to get...

When it comes to questions such as 'why do you want to work for this organisation' it is important to show that you understand the organisation and its ethos. Focus on what skills, drive and experience you will bring to the organisation, not just what the job will do for you. Ensure you communicate your passion for this particular organization, not just the field (although the two can be combined).

> *"I really want to work for the Smith Corporation because I know that you are a leader in the field of integrated micro-electroncs, and I have wanted to develop my career within that field since I left University. I'm aware that you have world class facilities, and are developing a range of new products, and I'd be excited to bring my own skills and experience to the projects that you are creating."*

Of course, in some circumstances the panel may be aware that the change of job is forced through redundancy etc, and in that case its best to acknowledge it, but then turn things round...

> *"My current position is being downsized due to a large-scale reorganisation, but I'm reframing that as a positive thing. I was*

starting to feel that I wanted a new challenge, and your position is ideal for my skills and will provide me with the challenge I'm looking for. Smith Corporation is someone I have wanted to work for for a long time, and I'd really like to make a difference to your organisation..."

One of the ways to enhance your answer to this question is to think of it from both your own perspective and that of the organisation. Many job applicants focus on a 'me' centred answer such as 'it's a great opportunity for me to further my career' etc. but at the end of the day the interviewer may be more interested in what you can do for them than what they can do for you. Make sure that you bring in enthusiasm for their organisation, and elements that are interesting and valuable to them, and create a win-win answer.

For example:

"I have always been aware of YourCorp and been interested in a career with you. I have a passion for making widgets, and with your focus upon that field and my experience in creating cutting edge widgets, I feel that this would be an exciting place for me to be. I feel that could bring my experience to complement your work in the widget field".

Now it's time to think about how you might answer this question. There are three elements to consider which can create a good order and structure, starting with your feelings about the organisation, and your enthusiasm for joining them. Then move on to what you bring them in terms of skills and experience, and finally the focus is back on you and how these fit into your overall career plan and trajectory.

Top Tips

- Ensure you really understand what the role and organisation are all about.
- Focus not just on what it can do for you, but also what you will bring them.

Question – "Why should we select you?"

An alternative version of this question is *'Why should we take you on?'*, and they can also sometimes load the question with more pressure through framing it as *'We have many applicants for this position, so why should be select you over the others?'*

This can be a bit of an uncomfortable question to answer because many people feel that it asks them to push themselves forward to an extent that they may be uncomfortable with. Also, there is an element of perceiving being asked to put down other applicants by rating yourself as better than them, which naturally many find challenging.

This leads to an interesting situation, as you are sitting there because you do feel that you would be ideal for the job and feel that you are a great candidate, but at the same time you don't want to say it!

Of course, an interview isn't a place to be too shy about your abilities, so say it you should. You need to be able to clearly highlight why you are the candidate they should choose. Fortunately, there are ways that it can be answered in a way that is both positive and shows a respect for the other candidates. Let us look at how you might do this…

People who are very aware of others and very social creatures often don't enjoy saying that they are better than other people, as possibly implied by the question. So, you can avoid this by simply and explicitly not doing so, by saying something on the lines of:

> *"Naturally I'm not in a position to comment upon other applicants, but I do feel that I am absolutely right for the position because…"*

A nice sidestep there. You are not critiquing others that are being interviewed, but at the same time you are saying confidently that you'd be a great fit to the job. Now, if you are using this, it is vital to then be very clear and explicit that you are the perfect fit to the post:

"...I do feel that I am absolutely right for the position because..."

Now you really need to drive home to the interviewer just why you are the right person for the job. This has got to be well aligned with their requirements for obvious reasons, so in your preparation take a good look at the job or person specification and decide what those key points of alignment are. The rule of three is good here, so ensure that you have three distinct and strong points you can make.

Give the interview examples of your positive achievements related to the requirements of the position to show that you can do the job well. You can reiterate one of your strengths here but use a different example of your using that strength. You can also bring in experience in the role and technical skills.

Because of the form of this question, it can be useful to directly reference what they are looking for:

"I understand that the applicant you are seeking for the position is somebody who will create and develop your new markets in the South of England for your products. In my current role I have expanded our core market by over 25% and created new sales opportunities across the country. I'm really passionate about what I do and want to create a marketing team that is the best in the business. I also feel that I'm really good at communicating and working with people — building bridges and making connections that pay off over the longer term..."

This question really does not have to be an uncomfortable one. Remember also, that confidence sells. If you don't put across that you believe that you are absolutely right for the position, then it will be a problem. After all, if you do not believe that you are right for it, then why should the interviewer?

Top Tips

- Really think about why you are right for the job.
- If uncomfortable about saying you are better than others, develop a sidestep answer.

Question – "What are your Strengths?"

This is one of the traditional and most important questions in interviews. It can come up in a variety of ways, from the straightforward 'What are your strengths' to the subtler 'What do you feel you will bring to the organisation' which can include other elements.

It's an important question, and even though it doesn't necessarily appear quite as often as it used to, the core elements of it will usually be probed in some way or another - after all interviews are all about finding out how what you offer is matched to the needs of the organisation. It's also crucial to go into your interview feeling confident, so reflecting upon your strengths is excellent preparation.

I would suggest preparing for this question in two parts. First, thinking about what your skills and strengths are, and how they might relate to the job or person specification. Then, in the second part, exploring how to structure an effective answer. By the way, although from here on I'll simply talk about strengths, in most cases skills and strengths can be used pretty much synonymously in interview. For instance, experience in computer programming can be both a skill and a strength, as can leadership qualities, etc.

As an aside, if your interviewer asks for what skills you bring to the organisation, experience isn't necessarily the same as ability. Extensive experience in leadership, for example, is not automatically a strength or skill - you may be experienced but still bad at it! If you are using, for example, leadership as a skill/strength, you need to demonstrate an example of effective leadership - where your leadership made a difference.

To begin, let's think about how many strengths you need. I feel that three well defined and evidenced strengths can work really well - the power of three. Some people like to mention more, but doing so could sound as if you are just throwing out a long list of random ideas, and hoping that something sticks in the mind of the interviewer. Three well referenced and supported strengths will usually work nicely…

Top Tip
- Three strengths are a good number to use.

Skills are often divided into soft and hard skills, but whether it is useful in interview preparation to think of it in this way, I am not convinced. Instead, let us consider what the role might needs, in three different domains, and work from there.

The domains that I would like to consider are firstly, our Social or People Skills, such as communication, empathy, and leadership. Secondly, there are our Personal Qualities and Inner Values such as our Work Ethic, Conscientiousness, Reliability etc. Finally, and crucially, there are our technical skills and experience, which can be job related trained skills such as accounting, computer programming languages. For many roles, one strength from each domain will make a powerful package and a strong answer.

Top Tips
- The domains of strengths are:
  - Social or People Skills
  - Personal Qualities and Inner Values
  - Technical Skills and Experience
- One from each can often be the basis of a strong answer.

Now, the strengths question is often quite an early and important question within the interview, so which strengths should you use? Think of it this way - this question is not really about your strengths as such, but about what you will bring to the position you are applying for within the organisation, so there will be certain things that they will be looking for.

You need to consider what these might be, and this is where the person and/or job specification come into play. Carefully studying this, you can get a good idea of the sorts of strengths that will be relevant and important to demonstrate. Obviously, you can talk about a whole range of different strengths, but if they aren't relevant to the position that you are interviewing for, then they won't be of great interest to the interviewer.

So, let's start to define your strengths that you might use. Jot down a list of your skills and strengths that come immediately to mind within the three areas. Don't worry if they are relevant to the job yet, just let your mind come up with as many possibilities as you can.

Now take your time and go back to your past work experiences, and think about what skills you have used and developed there – is there anything that you missed? Think about both different roles you undertook in the job and different situations you faced within those roles – what skills did you use effectively? Areas to consider are communication, interpersonal skills, technical skills, creative skills, problem solving etc. Add these to your list…

Now, refer to the list of skills and strengths that follows. It's not exhaustive – there are just too many possibilities – but it might give you ideas for anything obvious that you may have missed. Add anything important - however, make sure that these are your genuine key strengths. We need to focus, so don't just write down everything on the list – even if you are awesome!

- Communication
  o Verbal
  o Written

- Leadership
- Teamwork
- Self-Motivation
- Empathy
- Defusing Conflict
- Autonomy/Self Reliance
- Dealing with/Motivating People
- Reliability and Dependability
- Patience
- Persistence/Determination
- Resilience
- Persuasiveness
- Integrity/Trustworthiness
- Energy/ Enthusiasm
- Loyalty
- Work Ethic
- Organizational and Planning Skills
- Creativity
- Initiative
- Flexibility and Adaptability
- Decision-making and Judgment
- Problem Solving
- Gathering, Analysing and Managing Information

Finally, are there additional skills and strengths which you could legitimately claim to have after reviewing the job description and its requirements?

Look at the job specification and details, and highlight any skills from your list that you think that the job will need, such as being a team leader, problem solving skills, customer care etc.. If you are having difficulties choosing, perhaps start by considering one from each of the three domains – a people strength, a personal qualities strength, and a technical strength.

Now, how does that look? Do those three reflect the you that you want to project at interview?

Remember the psychological power of three, and make sure that you have chosen three really relevant strengths (having one from each domain is a good starting point, but sometimes it might be better to double up in one area – it depends on the role). Having done so, think of a good example where you have demonstrated each, and jot them down. This can be hardest for the soft skills such as 'good communication' but these are also the most important to demonstrate. Try not to use the same example for different skills as it can give the impression that your experiences and skills aren't diverse enough.

Make sure that you will have enough detail about not just the fact that you used the skill, but exactly how you applied it. Saying that you used your team leader skills is one thing, but what did you actually do?

Top Tip
- When putting together your list of three strengths, consider alignment to the role and person specification.

OK, so now let's think about delivering these strengths in a cohesive answer. The order to deliver them in the interview is in order of importance and relevance to the position you are applying for, as this will have the greatest impact. Thus, it's the most relevant or important to the role strength you should talk about first, then the second and so on…

Top Tip

- In your answer, lead with the most relevant and important strength for the role first.

Now, practice delivering these. What will you say, and how will you say it? It's good practice to segue straight from the strength into a short example, especially where it is a general and over-quoted skill such as 'good communication'. For example...

"One of my key strengths is that I'm a good communicator in teams. As an example, last month I was asked to lead my team in a new project and so had to communicate exactly what I needed from each individual, and I achieved that by ...."

This is not the time to be modest – don't undersell yourself, which it can be easy to do. Also, make sure you mention strengths which are quite focused and not too generalised. If you do look at generalised skills and strengths, then perhaps you could even apply them to the position at hand:

"I'm very organised, and I like to make sure that all the details are correct. This means that, in this role I believe that it would help me to ensure projects are bought in on time and under budget"

The interviewer will be looking for all of these when asking the question, although the balance of which are most important will, of course, depend upon the position you are applying for. Also, remember that although your qualifications and experience are already known from your CV, it can be worth reiterating key aspects of them.

Also, don't forget that this question can be asked in various ways, from the straightforward "What do you feel your strengths are?" through to the broader "What would you bring to the organisation?" which could include strengths as well as other factors.

So, now let's take a look at a fuller example:

"I think that I have a range of strengths that I would bring to the organisation to help ensure my success within the role. I feel that the key strengths that I bring would be, firstly, an ability to work under high levels of pressure and to meet very tight and rigid time deadlines whilst still bringing the team together and keeping the work atmosphere harmonious and productive – for example, I recently managed to bring a key customer focused initiative to completion in under 6 months while maintaining the highest levels of team morale. Secondly, I am highly motivated to do an excellent job – I have very high standards which I aim to reach at all times, for example ensuring that all the clients additional requests were successfully actioned in the recent project I was working on. Thirdly, my knowledge of the customer facing environment is excellent, as I have had 15 years' experience in a range of customer facing roles, dealing with people in many different situations and so am able to deal with any customer challenge effectively."

Top Tips
- Don't be too modest - they want to hear about your strengths so tell them about them.
- Make sure each strength can be backed up with a short example.

Question – "What are your Weaknesses?"

This is one of the questions many people dread, and it's not hard to understand why. Here you are in an interview, trying to project that image of high levels of competence and professionalism, and then they apparently ask you to allow them to peek behind the mask, and tell them what could be wrong with you as a potential employee! People feel, as they answer this question, as if they are giving the panel a great reason to turn them down. There is also ego involved, as admitting weakness is not on everyone's list of favourite things to do.

So, naturally we don't like to answer it, which means that, if we are not careful, we can produce a rather weak answer.

However, it is important to realise that it isn't necessarily the case that the interviewer is looking for reasons to be negative about you or reject you for the role. What the interviewer will be looking for instead is a level self-awareness, and a willingness and ability to overcome challenges and grow. After all, we are all human, and so we are all going to have weaknesses as well as strengths - if somebody said to you that they had no weaknesses, would you believe them? Probably not…

When I interview, it concerns me far more when applicants either don't seem to have any awareness of weaknesses, which could suggest a lack of reflection and self-awareness, or are really unwilling to mention them as this can show a lack of self-confidence and preparedness to deal with them. Like most interviewers, what I want to see when I interview is that level of personal awareness and authenticity, combined with an attitude of openness to personal development to overcome whatever the challenges are, and move forward.

Top Tip

- Remember this question isn't trying to fail you at the interview, but instead demonstrate your self-awareness.

Now today, with many organisations moving to an approach of a generally more positive interview process, this precise question will be heard less often. However, it will occur often enough that you do need to be ready for it with an effective answer. Everyone is human, and everyone has weak points, so don't let it throw you.

Although this question is obviously related to strengths, it is very different in terms of how we should answer it. We don't want to talk about a plethora of weaknesses, but neither is it wise to claim to have no weaknesses at all.

Now, there are really five possible ways of approaching this question, which can be summarised as:

- **The Weakness as a Strength**. Always a popular choice in interview answers is the weakness that can be reframed as a strength – for instance an excessive attention to detail can be reframed as being very useful to avoid errors in the workplace.
- **The Overcome Weakness** – Another classic approach is to talk about weakness that is relevant to the position which you used to have, but have now overcome, demonstrating both personal development and allowing you to talk about how you did this. Thus, although it was a weakness, it is one no more!
- **The Universal Weakness.** This is talking about a very common weakness that pretty much everyone has, including the interviewer so is unlikely to be considered problematic. Not often used in interview answers, and if used the weakness should not be one that impacts the role.
- **The Irrelevant Weakness** – admitting to a weakness that is completely unrelated to the position that you are interviewing for, and so wouldn't affect it. Again, not often used in interview.

- **The Honest Weakness.** A bit of a surprise to many people is that there is always the possibility of talking about an honest weakness that you have. This is an approach used by people either having quite a naïve approach, or alternatively, a very clever one, as authenticity and honesty can be powerful and effective in interview.

Top Tip
- There are five approaches to the weakness question - the most commonly used is the weakness as a strength, followed by the overcome weakness.

If asked about your weaknesses, talking about a single one is probably the way to go. Now, although I say that its best to only mention one, you should have more than one weakness prepared that you can talk about in case of a follow up question such as "Would you say that you had any other weaknesses?". This can be useful, as interviewers know that you will have prepared one as an answer to this question, and so may want to dig a bit more. It can give the wrong impression if you answer really well for one, but then can't think of anything else, as it will look as if you have prepared for this one rather than the answer being spontaneous and authentic.

Top Tip
- Prepare two weakness - one to use and one as a 'back-up'..

Decide which of the approaches you feel would work best for you and the interview, which will of course depend on the organisation and the position. For old fashioned organisations the weakness as a strength can work very well, although to be honest it is probably overused to the point of cliche. An organization that prides itself of staff development and a personal centred approach to its staff is more likely to relate to the way you overcome weakness as personal development etc...

For me, the overcome weakness is potentially the strongest as it combines honesty and openness, with self-awareness and a desire for self-improvement. Those elements should prove popular with many interviewers.

So, let's look at how we might answer the weakness question using the different approaches.

Firstly, The Weakness as a Strength. Now, as I mentioned, the Weakness as Strength has become a bit of a cliché, as it is used a lot. It's easy to see why as it gets around many of the problems of actually having a weakness, but because of this, interviewers are now more aware and likely to throw in a follow up, so be ready for that. However, if this is an approach that you feel will work for you, then give it a go! Let's take a look at a couple of examples:

> "I must admit I get frustrated when colleagues don't really contribute fully to projects – I'm passionate about what I do and getting things done its disappointing to me when others don't engage completely with something that is important that we are working on"

Or, how about:

> "Because I'm a team player, and want to support others in the team, I can sometimes have problems saying 'no' to colleagues…"

The overcome weakness can be quite an effective approach:

> "I used to find public speaking, such as giving presentations, really challenging. I would get very nervous, but I've been working

on building my confidence, and I feel that I'm now able to do public speaking without it being a problem."

"One of my main challenges was a tendency to try to multitask too much to get everything done quickly. I have found that by developing more efficient time management, I can now focus to complete tasks more effectively whilst still juggling others."

"I found my timing on projects was challenging – I tended to leave things a bit too close to deadline, but I have got a new approach of starting projects earlier, and planning out the workflow…"

The universal weakness is less often used…

"Like many people I find public speaking, such as giving presentations to large audiences really challenging and I get really nervous. It's something that I would like to work on and build my confidence in this area…"

As mentioned earlier, the stated weakness should not be one that seriously impacts the role. In this example of public speaking, someone going for a lecturer role might find it problematic!

The irrelevant weakness is admitting to a weakness that is completely unrelated to the position that you are interviewing for, and so wouldn't affect it.

"Well, if I'm honest, working with figures has never been my strongest point. I did really well at college in English, and I'm great communicating and talking to people, but Maths and figure-work isn't my strongest area, unfortunately."

OK, so you can see what we have done there. Maths isn't the key to the position on offer, so the weakness is unimportant to the interviewer. But there's something else, we have also put forward a strength that is relevant in a way that seems natural in the context of the answer. English is more likely to be relevant to the sales position and so mentioning it can be effective in pushing a strength even here…

The honest weakness is a bit of a surprise to many people, but there is always the possibility of talking about an honest weakness that you have. This can be powerful, as it shows an openness and authenticity that many interviewers will find refreshing. But, it is a high risk strategy and I think that there is still a need to be a little circumspect with the choice of weakness. So, nothing too extreme…

> "Like many people I find public speaking, such as giving presentations, really challenging and I get really nervous. It's something that I would like to work on and build my confidence in this area…"

> "People who aren't team players and won't listen I do find frustrating to work with and it's something I'm working on".

> "To be honest, I really need to develop my knowledge of property law further. It's an area I'm very interested in, but haven't managed to go into enough depth to satisfy me"

> "One of the challenges that I face is that I'm pretty uncomfortable taking risks"

So, it's a good time to define the weaknesses that you might use. Take some time to think about two weaknesses you may use. There is a list of some common possibilities below for ideas, but this is only illustrative and isn't exhaustive. Have an example of two that you'd be comfortable to talk about in the interview – you are unlikely to need them but just in case!...

• I focus too much on the details

- I have an inability to delegate.
- I put too much responsibility on myself
- I have trouble saying "no."
- Impatience when projects run beyond the deadline
- I could use more experience in…
- I sometimes lack confidence
- Have trouble asking for help
- Working with certain personalities
- Maintaining a healthy work/life balance
- Uncomfortable with ambiguity
- Wanting to Please Everyone
- Self-criticism.
- Shyness.
- Public speaking.
- Taking Negative Criticism.
- I'm sometimes a bit too much of a details/big picture person…
- I can find it challenging to work with people who aren't as driven as me/don't listen to others/ try to take over…
- If I've personally initiated and developed a project, it can be really difficult for me to let go and hand it on to someone else
- I tend to be risk averse…
- I can be disorganised at times…

Top Tip
- Think about the weaknesses relevance to the role - will it affect it?

Answering 'Left Field' Questions

Interviews have fashions, just as with so many other aspects of life. One of the well-known interview fashions - though less used than it used to be - is the idea of 'left field' questions. These are questions designed to make you think on the spot, and which often have no obvious correct answers.

There are actually two main types of the left field question. There is the estimator type, in which the interviewer asks you a question such as *'How many people could fit in St Paul's Cathedral?'*. The idea of this one is to get a feel of how good you are at estimating or calculating on the fly. They can tend to be more used in technical type roles.

The other type is the really challenging or unanswerable question. Something such as *'How would you describe the colour orange to a blind person?'* would be an example of this. There is no right answer, instead the interest is in how you will tackle the topic and the flexibility and insight of your answer.

So why do these types of questions exist? Well, just think about it for a moment. What are you currently doing, but developing and rehearsing interview answers to the questions that could arise? Thus, your answers may therefore not actually reflect you and your true potential, but instead how well you have rehearsed.

Now that does tell the interviewer something about you, and how seriously you are taking the interview, but perhaps not enough for their liking. They want to know how you really think when you haven't had time to prepare, and hence we get the 'left field' question. It is a question that you probably won't have thought of and hence will not have had chance to prepare, as there are so many possibilities you can't practice them all, and the interviewer can easily come up with their own additional questions.

So, this is a genuinely challenging interview question, and can give an important insight into how you think. It can also be thought of as a type of reasoning or intelligence test.

So, why do people use them less today? Well, perhaps one reason is because the answer can be so varied it can be difficult to score – particularly judging and comparing between candidates. After all, consider when questions such as *'If you were a biscuit, what type of biscuit would you be, and why?'* became very popular. The idea is to get you to think on your feet and demonstrate your true abilities rather than delivering pre-prepared answers, and it could be good at that. But the challenge is that answers to questions such as these then must be scored subjectively, which can be somewhat challenging and inconsistent. Was saying that you were a 'Bourbon' biscuit better than claiming to be a 'Rich Tea'?..

Because of this, and the need for hiring decisions to be seen to be fair (and defensible in case of challenge) many have generally gone back to an older style of more standard questions and competency or strength based interviews – after all, could you really say as an interviewer that you denied someone a job because they had described themselves as a Chocolate Hobnob? Probably not...

However, be aware that there are still organisations that use questions such as this, so we will explore them, but they tend to be rarer and applied in certain organisations and situations – cool tech companies and the like still seem to be the most likely to use them.

So, assuming that they might come up, let's consider how they might be answered. The most important element to be aware of is that what is crucial to the interviewer is not the final answer, but the thinking process you use to get there. That's what they are really interested in. Remember back to maths exams in school or college, where you were told to show your working as they gave marks or that even if you got the wrong answer? Well, with left field questions there often is no single right answer so it's all about the working – your thought process!

Top Tip
- Answering these questions is more about how you think about and work out an answer, rather than getting the 'right' answer.

Since there are so many possibilities, we'll just look at a couple to give you a feel of one way of answering them.

Firstly, what I think of as a calculation question, and we'll use the one that I suggested earlier – "How many people could fit in St Paul's Cathedral?" …

The first thing is to be aware of assumptions. What do they mean – in terms of fitting people in the floor area, or do they mean volume if you could stack people on top of each other? Remember this is about thinking so logical realism isn't important.

So, you should perhaps give an answer that states you have noticed the ambiguity and covers both possibilities…

"Well, if we are just talking about how many people we could fit into the floor, I think that St Pauls is about 150m long by 40m wide, which gives us 6000 square metres. If we can fit three people a square meter, that means we could get 18,000 people in the main part, plus the two apses are about 20m square giving us a total of another 800 square metres so that's another 2400 people Overall then, a first approximation would be 20,400 people, although that would be pretty cosy!

Of course, if we could stack people, as I'd estimate it's probably about 50m high and people are about 2m tall, we could multiply that by 25, so about 500,000 people if we filled the volume!..."

You can see here the way the thought process is demonstrated. Is the answer numerically correct? Almost certainly not, but that is not so important. Instead, the willingness to have a go and, crucially, demonstrate a logical process.

How about the other, more conceptual, question, such as 'How would you describe the colour orange to a blind person?'. Well here its again about process, but this time it's about approaching the problem in a novel way. Don't get hung up on trying to find the single right answer – there isn't one. Instead come up with what you can and explain your thoughts clearly…

"Well, that's a really interesting question. I think that I wouldn't try to describe the colour orange in visual terms, as they don't have a useful reference. Instead, I might say to them that if colours were music, then orange would be a tune that most people think of as cheerful and happy. It's a bright tune, and one that stands out even when there are other tunes around…"

So, if you do get one of these questions – don't panic! Think of an answer and go for it, explaining your process as you go!

To help prepare for these types of questions, have a go at the two below. Make notes about how you'd go about it…

1) *How many square metres of pizza are eaten in the UK every year? …*

2) *If your life was a TV programme, which one would it be and why?*

Introduction to Competency Questions

One of the most encountered question formats is that of competency-based questions. In these, you are asked to provide an example of what you have done in the past. You will therefore get questions with the basic question structure of:

> *"Can you give us an example of when you made a challenging decision?"*

Or

> *"Tell us about a time when you overcame a challenge"*

There are a couple of key elements to be remembered about competency questions. The first is that you need good examples to use. This is, of course, obvious but many people tend to leave thinking about examples until they are in the interview room, at which point their mind goes blank! Hence, it is important to think of some excellent examples ahead of time.

Secondly, you really need a range of different situations as your examples. Using the same situation for many different questions can suggest a lack of breadth of experience, and ideally you should use a different example for every question. Of course, having said that, if in the heat of the interview you cannot recall a different good example you might re-use an earlier example, although you may want to qualify this:

> *"I mentioned before about when I communicated effectively, but I feel that situation was also a good example of when I made a challenging decision. The situation was..."*

I mentioned earlier that you need a range of examples. Personally, I recommend looking at a range of areas rather than just focusing on particular possible questions. If you simply rehearse a specific question, and something a little different comes up, it can be difficult to change your answer to match the question effectively. If, however, you have thought about the examples of what you have done in different and commonly explored domains, then it can be easier to fit them into the individual questions as they arise.

So, what areas might you need examples of? Once again, it rather depends on the role - for example if you are going for a role that involves you being part of a team, the competency question may ask about being a team member, whereas a team leadership or management role will question your leadership experience.

Some possibilities of areas to consider, if they are likely to form part of the role you are applying for, are:

- Effective Communication or Influence
- Teamwork, or Leading a Team
- Dealing with Conflict
- Overcoming a Challenge/Problem Solving
- An Innovative Approach
- Making an Important Decision
- Working to a Tight Deadline
- Supporting Change
- Building/Maintaining Relationships with Colleagues / Customers / Stakeholders
- Resilience
- Going the Extra Mile
- Demonstrating Adaptability/Flexibility

This is by no means an exhaustive list but should give you a starting point to think about what behaviours they may be interested in, and make sure that you have examples ready to go.

Top Tips
- Think about a range of appropriate examples you can use in likely competency questions.

Often, when answering a competency type question, we need to give an example of what we have done or a situation that we have encountered. A classic question here would be "Tell us about a time that you dealt with a difficult customer".

Now let's take a look at what to include in your competency answer.

There are good ways of answering this question, and not so good ways... Consider this answer to a question about dealing with a challenging customer...

> "I think that one occasion where I dealt with a challenging customer was when I was working at SmithCo. There was a gentleman that was really angry. He came into the office – I think it was a Wednesday, or possibly it might have been a Thursday. I think that it was raining too – it was a pretty miserable day. He was really angry because he had received two really different quotes from us. He's spoken to my colleagues, and they hadn't helped the situation. So he came in, and I had just got back from lunch. So I spoke to him and calmed him down. I think that I handled it really well..."

There's a lot of detail here, which might be thought a good thing. However, it tells us little about the real meat of the question, <u>how</u> you dealt with the challenging customer... You see, the interviewer is asking about something that happened to you, and so you might be tempted to give them the full and detailed story about what happened but, perhaps somewhat surprisingly, the interviewer may not be very interested in details of the story itself!

Instead, what they want to know is what you did and why you did it. What did you consider? What did you actually do? Why did you take that course of action?

I think of this as 'process', as opposed to 'story', and the two are quite different. I have found that so many people tend to give too much detail of the story, and very little detail on their process. Think about the example we have just looked at, what does the interviewer really know about you and how you would actually deal with an angry customer from this? How much is relevant to what they want to know? Actually, very little.

One way to think of it is that story are the unique details of what happened to you, whilst process are those things you would tell someone to do in a similar situation.

For instance, take this possible competency answer about dealing with an angry customer...

"I was working at BurgerMatic, the fast food outlet. I had worked there about 6 months and it was the first job I had managed to get after college. I was on the late shift... or perhaps it was the early shift. I had torn my uniform that morning and it was really busy. It was also really warm, and my workmates were all complaining as they had to work extra hours. I think that we were short staffed at the time as some people had been fired for not working hard. We had a new line of burgers that was proving to be really popular, so the queues were quite long as everyone was buying this burger with extra cheese and lettuce in it. This burger came in a special blue wrapper with red writing on it. And this guy came in an ordered a cheeseburger, and I think he had fries as well, but he was really unhappy at having to wait for the fries to be cooked and so started to give one of my *colleagues a hard time. So I calmed him down and gave him a fruit pie for free."*

OK, so this is a bit tongue in cheek, but to be honest it's not far off what many people do in interview – lots of detail of the story, but very little about their process. Remember, the interviewer doesn't really care about the burger, or the colour of its wrapper. Instead, what they are interested in is how you dealt with the situation, as that is what you may have to do in the role they are interviewing you for…

So, let's take a look at a more process-focused answer.…

"I was working at BurgerMatic, the fast food outlet. I had worked there about 6 months and it was the first job I had managed to get after college. We were short staffed at the time, and we had a new line of burgers that was proving to be really popular so the queues were quite long. A customer came in and ordered, but because we were busy and short staffed he had a long wait and began to get angry. He started to raise his voice to one of my colleagues, and I decided that it was important to deal with the situation, as my colleague was new to the role and inexperienced. I approached the customer and asked him why he was unhappy, and listened to him as he told me he was in a hurry, and that this was a fast food joint that wasn't! It's important to listen to really understand the situation before trying to solve the problem, so I calmly listened to the customer, which showed him respect but also a chance to calm down. Then I explained calmly the situation and apologised with him. I wanted to keep a loyal customer, so when he had calmed down, he did apologise to me for getting irate, and I added a free fruit pie to his order as an additional way of apologising, and the customer left actually smiling, which was great."

Perhaps you can see that here we have more detail about what you considered, what you did, and why – your process for dealing with a situation. This will give the interviewer more confidence that you can handle that type of scenario. It can still more detailed, depending upon what the situation and role is, but the core idea is to remember more details about what you did and why, and not just talk about the story around it - the story is merely a frame for your thoughts and actions, which is what the interviewer will want to know about.

Now, this is general advice. There are some people who are natural raconteurs, who can tell a story in a way which is totally enthralling, and they can often get away with more story, and even use it to their advantage to gain rapport with the interviewer. However, unless this is you, then play it safe and ensure that you talk more about your process than the fine background details…

Top Tip
- Remember to focus on your process when giving your example, not irrelevant story details.

Competency Questions - Using STAR and SITAR

Let's face it, in the heat of the interview, the pressure is on for us to come up with great answers. However, keeping a clear head under pressure can be challenging, so it can be good to have something to fall back on to help us structure your answers when things get tough.

This is where, for many people, an acronym can be useful, as they help us to remember and communicate information more easily. Under pressure, we need to recall how to effectively structure our answer, and an acronym can really help here.

Using 'STAR'

A mnemonic can help us remember a good structure that we can than fold our answer around. So, let's start with one of the most popular – one you'll see mentioned almost everywhere when interviews are discussed…

If you've been doing any research into interview preparation, you will probably have come across the acronym STAR. STAR is a popular way of answering some questions in the interview situation, especially in a competencies interview, as it gives you a structure that you can develop your answer around.

Remember, competency questions are those that ask for an example of what you have done in the past and so using the STAR format would give the following structure…

The 'S' in STAR stands for situation. What was the situation in which you faced this challenge or exhibited this behaviour or response?

The 'T' is for Task, which is what your role, or task, was in the situation. What task were you responsible for?

The 'A' is Action – what you actually did to deal with the situation – basically your response.

The 'R' is the Result. What was the actual outcome of your actions?

Using the acronym like this helps you to structure your answer and ensure that you not only answer the question fully but also give a better response that explains more about your process. Let's take a look at how it might be applied. Let's suppose the interviewer has asked you about a time when you overcame a particular challenge.

Using the star approach, you might say something such as:

> *"In my previous career there was an extremely tight deadline for a really large project (Situation). I was team leader, and so my role was to make sure that the project got delivered on time, and also meet the brief we had been given (Task) In order to make sure that we hit the deadline I broke down what we needed to do and distributed the task elements between the team members based on what I saw to be their skills and experience, so each could focus upon one section and so make sure that it was completed on time (Action). Doing this meant that we actually managed to complete the project within the overall time frame and still keep it under budget overall. (Result)."*

This is a pretty solid structure and works pretty well for a lot of interviews. If you are new to interviews, or you want a simple easy structure, then this could be the best approach for you.

By the way, although STAR gives a structure to deliver an answer that works well, it's ok to alter the order of the elements. Particularly, you may wish to put the task before the situation if you feel that gives a better answer for you.

Top Tip
- The STAR format is a classic structure for interview answers.

However, I feel that STAR often misses out an element that can make a big enhancement to the impression that you give. For me, contextualising more clearly why the situation was important in the bigger picture can really add something to your answer, by demonstrating a big picture awareness, so let's explore an addition to STAR that might help you do this...

Using 'SITAR'

To explore this idea, let's turn our STAR into a SITAR... It's easy to remember the acronym by thinking of the wonderful and melodic Indian musical instrument!

As before, the STAR part remains that same, but now we add in 'I' for importance, making the structure:

The 'S' in SITAR stands for situation. What was the situation in which you faced this challenge or exhibited this behaviour or response?

We now have 'I' for importance or impact of this to the team, organisation and/or customer.

The 'T' is for Task, which is what your role, or task, was in the situation. What task were you responsible for?

The 'A' is Action – what you actually did to deal with the situation – basically your response.

The 'R' is the Result. What was the actual outcome of your actions?

Let's see how this enhances our previous answer.

> *"In my previous career there was an extremely tight deadline for a really large project (Situation). This project was crucial for the organisations success as it would really raise our profile and so enable us to win more key clients, and allow us to expand (Importance) I was team leader, and so my role was to make sure that the project got delivered on time, and also met the brief we had been given (Task) In order to make sure that we hit the deadline I broke down what we needed to do and distributed it between the team members based on what I saw to be their skills and experience, so each could focus upon one section and so make sure that it was completed on time (Action). Doing this meant that we actually managed to complete the project within the overall time frame and still keep it under budget overall. (Result)."*

You see, what we are doing here is to show that we don't just focus upon our own interests within the organisation but are also thinking on a higher more organisational level and about impact on others and the big picture.

Now some people will naturally have added this importance element into the Situation (S) element of STAR, but I have found that it certainly isn't usual enough to rely on people to do that.

So, if the role you are going for requires that level of wider awareness, and you want to demonstrate it in your answers, then playing the SITAR might just work for you...

Top Tip
- The SITAR format develops more depth than STAR, and can work even better when answering many interview questions.

Competency Question – "Can you give us an example of when you communicated effectively?"

This is a classic interview question. Communication skills are an integral part of most jobs, so the interviewer will want to know that you have thought about how you communicate, and also have demonstrated an ability to communicate effectively. Ensure you talk about how you communicated - what did you consider in your approach to your communication?

There are many aspects to communication, including:
- Tone of voice.
- Listening skills.
- Words used.
- Technical/accessible communication.
- etc

Example

> *"I believe that I communicate very effectively in a wide range of situations. I think a good example was when I was working as an estate agent, negotiating between vendors and buyers of property [Task]. In that role I had to work with a wide range of people using effective communication as a tool to attract people into properties, as well as communicating both verbally and in writing to negotiate between buyers and sellers of property - often having to communicate complex information such as the reasons for legal difficulties and holdups to non-specialists.*
>
> *For example, I remember one particular instance where a person was purchasing a property and there were usage restrictions. I had to communicate with the vendors solicitor to fully understand the situation, before communicating this effectively and accurately to the buyer to explain the technical details as the legal situation*

was surprisingly complex [Situation]. It was important to keep the sale on track to get the commission, as well as provide a good and successful transaction for both buyer and seller [Importance].

Of course, there are different modes of communication, and felt in this case that it was better to have a face to face meeting with the buyer rather than telephone or email. It can be more effective to see and understand how the buyer was taking what I was telling them. I met with them and also used diagrams and a map of the property and its land to show the complexities of the situation. I took some time to explain by laying out the background the situation before explaining the particular obstacle that was in the way [Actions].

Having explain the situation to the buyer ensured they really understood it come on I found buyers still wanted to purchase the property but wanted to make a revised lower offer. This again required communication skills to communicate this to the vendor of the property explaining exactly why the buyer was making this offer. Eventually after communicating extensively with, and between, both sides, I managed to find the common ground that was required in order to successfully hold the sale together [Result].

I think in this situation I communicated in a number of different ways and achieved an outcome which was good for all parties."

Top Tip
- Ensure that you add in the methods and considerations behind how you communicated.

Competency Question – "Could You Give Us an Example of When You Made a Challenging Decision?"

This is not a common question, but may be encountered for some roles, especially in management etc. The answer should include how you considered the options - perhaps elements of risk and reward - and then arrived at your decision. Was it a bold decision, and why? What was the outcome?

Example

> *"Well certainly, I think a good example that springs to mind of when I made a challenging decision about an in-house software development project, when I had to decide whether to continue work on it, or not. [Situation]*
>
> *It was a challenging decision as we had key workflows tied up in the project, and also there were key cost implications and timescale issues in terms of needing to get the software up and running to support our organisations processes. [Importance] I was team leader, and the challenging decision was due to another piece of software that had just come onto the market that had most, but not all, of the functions that we needed. [Task]*
>
> *Switching would save time, but perhaps limit its usefulness to our staff. To make an effective decision, first of all I considered the different elements that both packages offered in terms of functionality. I explored with our end users which would be most useful, and also took into account the cost of the outside software verses the development cost of our own. After weighing up all these factors, I decided that the external software wouldn't quite do the job that we wanted to do, despite it's lower cost and that it could be deployed immediately, rather than the delay that would*

be caused by retaining our own project. So, I decided to continue our in-house development [Actions].

The software was delivered, and proved very effective at meeting our in-house users needs, far more than the alternate software would have done [Result]"

Competency Question – "Can You Give Us An Example Of Building Relationships With Others?"

This is quite a common question, and may be focused around building relationships in the workplace with team members, customers or other stakeholders.

It is important to not only give an example, but also to explain your approach - the key building blocks of relationship building - that you use. These are often elements such as:

- Communication
- Listening
- Respect
- Trust
- Reliability
- Empathy

Example

"When I initially worked for my current employer, I was employed as a company representative [Task]. I therefore worked closely with both the customers of our products and our suppliers as well. When I first took up the position, I decided to really try to build a more effective relationship with both groups. I wanted to build resilience into our relationship with our suppliers to ensure that we received timely deliveries which needed an improved relationship with them, and also to better understand my customers' needs [Situation].

I set up meetings with representatives of our suppliers, and the first thing that I did was to just listen to them — their concerns and the challenges they faced. I also encourage them to list any difficulties they had had regarding their dealing with our company. It transpired that our suppliers felt that we were slow paying their invoices, which in turn made these suppliers less amenable to any last-minute changes that we made to our order. That impacted upon the reliability of our supplying our product to our core customers, as the just-in-time ordering process meant that if we didn't receive the materials we need, then we would be delayed in supplying our customers [Importance].

I therefore realised that by solving one problem we would be able to improve relationships with both our suppliers and provide a more reliable service for our customers. I talked to the accounts department, and also management, and emphasised the importance of timely paying of the accounts, as this would then lead to potentially greater profitability. It took a while, but eventually I was able to ensure that accounts were paid promptly, which really enhanced our standing with our suppliers and really enhanced our relationship with them. I communicated my thanks to them for their patience in the past and assured them that the new situation would continue. I also gave kudos to the accounts department, as recognition and acknowledgement can make a huge difference to relationships [Action].

The outcome was that our supply chain became more reliable, which allowed an increase in sales to customers [Results]."

Competency Question – "Can You Tell Us About When You Overcame a Challenge?"

This is a very common question. Employers want resourceful people who will be able to deal with the challenges that the role puts their way.

With this question you need to have a very clear structure. Define what the challenge was, and why it was a challenge, before clearly defining your thought process and steps taken to overcome it. The (successful) outcome is also important to include.

Example

> "I feel that I have had excellent experience in overcoming many different challenges throughout my career.
>
> I think one very good example was when I was tasked with creating a new website for our organisation [Situation]. The challenge that I faced was that we had an extremely limited budget, but needed a website that would work well to attract customers [Importance].
>
> I considered the challenge and realised that the budget meant that we couldn't afford to have the website constructed by an outside company. Hence, to overcome this challenge we would have to produce it in-house, and the best way of doing this was by doing some of the work myself.
>
> To achieve this, it required learning website creation and design. By doing this, and so saving money on creating the core of the website, it meant that what little budget we had could then be spent upon the graphical elements which I felt were a key to really grabbing people's attention [Actions].

Doing it this way I managed to overcome the challenge of the limited budget, and create a really excellent website at a particularly advantageous cost [Results] ."

Competency Question – "Could You Give Us An Example Of When You Led A Team?"

This is a very common question for any leadership roles. It is important in answering this question to emphasize the importance of team leadership and how you did it, as well as giving an actual example.

They will be interested in your style of leadership, and how this affected your team. How did you build morale and relationships within the team? How did you create a focus upon goals etc? There is a lot to talk about with this one...

Example

> *"As a team leader I think it's really important to build a really positive team, as by doing that not only do you create a more harmonious working environment, but it also helps to reduce staff turnover meaning team stability and increases productivity and effectiveness.*
>
> *I think a good example of my team leadership was when I was working for a news website, and I was a team leader with a team of nine people [Task]. Our task was to develop a new online information portal covering a technical area [Situation].*
>
> *When I took over the team morale was at a low as unfortunately the previous team leader had been quite a negative and challenging personality and had reduced the teams morale to a low level. I realised that this needed to be quickly addressed to increase productivity and reduce potential staff turnover [Importance] and felt that the first step towards this was to create clear distinctions between their previous team leader and myself.*

To achieve this, I started by having one to ones with each team member to really get to know them, understand their skills, and to learn what challenges that they felt they faced both individually and as a team. This would help ensure that the team felt that they were being listened to and help build positive relationships with them.

After doing this it became clear that I had an excellent team and so I began to move forward by clearly redefining our goals for the main project we were tackling, as a clear sense of direction and a clear goal helps the team gel. It was a large challenge, so I started by breaking our main aim down to a series of sub goals that the team would feel was achievable, with each team member assigned tasks to suit their particular skills and experience. Then I ensured that as each team member completed a task I gave them praise and acknowledgement because by doing this people feel their work is valued and it enables them to really engage with new tasks [Actions].

Within a few weeks it was obvious that the team was now moving forward, as morale levels were much higher and productivity also extremely high. The team actually became very high functioning, and actually won an award for its innovative and exciting website which way I feel was due to the team being able to be productive and feel supported [Result].

I believe that I led the team effectively, building a positive atmosphere and also increasing productivity greatly."

Competency Example – "Could You Give Us An Example Of When You Dealt With Conflict?"

This is a very common question for any many roles - from customer facing roles dealing with challenging customers to management or team leadership and intervening in employee or team member conflict.

It is important in answering this question to emphasize the importance of resolving the conflict to the situation and organisation, and how you did it, as well as simply giving a good well-structured example. Of course, you should show how you decisively dealt with it, and it is important to use an example where you actually resolved the conflict, rather than simply avoiding the situation - for instance by reassigning one of the participants to another team.

It is also important to talk about your process for deciding your strategy, and any tools you used (for example tone of voice), etc?

Top Tip
- Make sure you talk about your process - what did you do, and why?

There are a number of elements that you might think about including within your answer to demonstrate that you understand conflict as well as being able to deal with it:
- That some conflict is natural and indeed, often inevitable.
- The importance of listening and understanding the reasons for the conflict. Often, conflict is created by misunderstanding or lack of communication.
- Staying calm and logical yourself - not lettings your emotions get involved.

- The importance of dealing effectively with the conflict, not passively hoping it will resolve itself.
- The importance of finding win-win situations where possible.
- Whenever possible, be positive not punitive.
- Your strategies, such as tone of voice etc.
- Being clear in your expectations of future behaviour.
- Be aware of formal procedures you could use if required.

Top Tip

- Demonstrate your understanding of conflict - that it is natural, the need to find win-win situations etc.

So, let's take a look at an example. It uses the SITAR format, but with the task coming first.

"[Task] I think a really good example of when I dealt with conflict occurred when I worked at RRT Electronics. I was team leader in charge of a small team designing a new consumer electronics product.

[Situation] I had two team members in my team who had an obvious personality clash. This was spilling into and affecting the workplace, which was obviously not acceptable. The problem was that, because of their personalities, they could never agree on how to achieve the goals they were set.

[Importance] To deliver the project on time it was essential that they worked together, so I realized that it was going to cause difficulties for the project, as well as the individuals involved. If I couldn't resolve their conflict, it would lead to time and budget over-runs. Their conflict was not only impacting upon the development of the new product but also creating bad feeling within the wider team.

[Actions] There are different approaches to dealing with conflict and in this situation, I felt that a subtler approach was called for rather than just 'reading the riot act'. It's really important to understand the basis of any conflict before you intercede, as if you interject in the wrong way you can make the situation worse. Therefore, the first thing I did was to meet both individuals in one-to-one meetings to try to understand the situation and what was behind the conflict between them. In this case the two team members had different backgrounds and been trained in different approaches which suggested to them different ways of doing things, and both assumed that their way was the most efficient. Hence doing things their colleague's way would slow the project as they saw it.

I decided that the best way to resolve the conflict was by giving each clear areas of responsibility, which did not overlap, and which allied with their individual skills and experience. With this as a solution to this conflict I then met both together and explored with them the higher order importance of them working together. I stated that I understand that they disagreed on methods and approaches, but the effect of their disagreement outweighed any possible efficiency losses through using one team members approach over another.

By keeping calm, listening, and using logical arguments I showed how each would have clear domains where they would be in charge, and they agreed. Then as the project went forward, I made sure that I praised the joint progress.

[Results] I found that, as I planned, the conflict reduced over time as they started to work together more effectively, and actually in the end became a harmonious team."

Competency Question – "Can You Tell Us About A Time When You Came Up With An Innovative Solution?"

This is a question that will occasionally surface for some roles. The interviewer will be looking for an example where you really looked at a situation or challenge afresh and though of a new way of tackling it. For many roles, the more innovative the example the better! Also, stressing the positive outcome of your innovative approach is important here.

Example

> "I think that a good example of an innovative solution I devised was when I was assistant manager at an underused leisure centre [Task]. My manager gave me the objective of increasing awareness and usage of the centre and increase the number of memberships that we had [Situation]. My manager had a concern that if usage didn't improve, the company that owned the centre could potentially close it, losing local people the facility, as well as everyone working there losing their jobs [Importance] .
>
> I was quite new to the role so the first thing that I did was to review everything that had been done previously. The centre had tried all the expected techniques the in the past, such as special rate offers, two for ones and so on, but they hadn't worked effectively enough and so I realised that I need to come up with something different and innovative to make a difference and really reach potential members.
>
> Talking to people in the community, I realised that many people saw exercise as a chore, and not enjoyable, so I decided that I needed to create an association with the centre being fun rather than leisure and gym activity seeming to be hard work. We also needed a higher profile.

So, I decided to be innovative and try something new. I got a couple of local celebrities who themselves used the centre and created an 'It's a Knockout' type contest with them as team captains, and with free admission for spectators. I combined this with a one-day sign-up offer as I hoped that the good feelings that the visitors had would ensure they were more likely to sign up, and I needed to help them decide [Actions].

It worked really well. At the end of the day, we had a audience of 800 people, many of whom had not visited the centre before, and 150 actually signed up as new members, most of whom did then come along and use the facilities. My bosses were really pleased, and they actually used the same technique at some other centres they owned [Result]."

Competency Question – "Could You Give Us An Example Of When You Worked To A Tight Time Deadline?"

This is a question that will occasionally surface for quite a few different roles. The interviewer will want to know that you can deal with possibly complex problems under time pressure. There are therefore a few different elements to keep in mind for this which they may be looking for:

- Ability to prioritise.
- Ability to multitask.
- Ability to work efficiently and so get a lot done quickly.

If your answer can explicitly include these it will be far stronger, and should also include your process - for instance what did you consider when prioritising, and why was that?

Example

"In my career I've had many occasions when I've had to work to an extremely tight time deadline. I have found that achieving successful outcomes under time pressure is about being organised, having clear goals, and breaking the task down into achievable sections.

One example of when I worked under a tight time deadline that I'd like to share is when I was creating an in-house magazine for my company. We had some important changes of organisational direction that management wanted to ensure everyone in the staff was aware of, and that they could see the benefits from, to ensure maximum buy-in by the workforce [Situation/Importance].

The inhouse magazine I was asked to create was a key element of this communication strategy, and obviously it was important that it was created and distributed ahead of the organisational changes that it introduced and covered in depth. My role, as part of the companies' communications team, was to pull together the text, images and design the layout [Task].

However, management only decided to create this magazine very late in the day, and so I only had three weeks to create the content because it had to go to the printers and be back and distributed within 6 weeks. When I'm under time pressure, the first thing I like to do is to ensure that I'm aware of everything that has to be done, so to make sure I would do things efficiently I mapped out the whole creation process – how much writing was needed, the images I needed to complement the text and so on. This ensured that I wasn't so focused in one part of the project I neglected another and ran out of time. Having checked out what needed to be done, I then reviewed the resources I had available, in term of existing copy, images etc, as well as other team members who could assist me in reaching my deadline.

I then broke the tasks required into different elements and handed them out according to the skills and experience of the other team members, and for my own work timeline it so I know how much I could spend on each part – although I did allow a bit of buffer time for unforeseen circumstances cropping up. Once I gathered the materials, I did a first draught and laid out so I could see what it looked like and could decide what images and additional materials were needed - I think it's important to keep reviewing progress and recognise possible shortfalls and problems. Although we were under extremely tight time constraints it was also really important that it was both accurate and hit the brief, so I requested others to review the materials to see whether the tone and content was both clear and engaging [Actions].

At the end of the day the magazine was produced within the time constraints, and management were extremely pleased with what we had created and the way that it helped introduce the key changes that we were making across the organisation really effectively [Result] ."

Competency Question – "Can You Give Us An Example of When You Demonstrated Resilience?"

This is a question that will occasionally surface for some roles. The interviewer will want to know that you can deal with pressure, while maintaining focus and productivity.

However, resilience is about not only being able to take pressure, but being able to bounce back after problems or setbacks. It encompasses not being discouraged when challenges emerge, or there appears to be a lack of progress etc. Hence, acknowledging challenges but staying focused and positive can be a key aspect of resilience that the interviewer may be looking for.

Some of the aspects of resilience that you may wish to include within your answer are:
- Ability to deal with pressure.
- Ability to bounce back after setbacks.
- Learning from setbacks and problems.
- Remaining positive and focused.

Top Tip
- Remember that resilience is not only about dealing with stress, but also bouncing back after setbacks and remaining positive and focused.

In the example below, all of the points in the list above are utilised.

Example

> *"[Situation] I think that a good example of my resilience was when I was a design technician, and part of a team undertaking product design.*

[Task] We were developing a new electronic consumer product, and under a lot of time pressure. We were constantly having major and unexpected setbacks in the project, meaning that it was both physically exhausting with long days (and weekends) and also psychologically challenging as these problems, at times, almost made it feel as if we would never succeed.

[Actions] However, I feel that I have inner strength to deal with challenges, and I realised that my resilience was crucial to see the project through to completion. To achieve this, I kept my focus upon the end goal, and ensured that I focussed on the idea that I was overall always moving forward - even a setback could be reframed as a lesson learned and an opportunity to do better.

Completing this project meant working long hours, but I also ensured that although I did go above and beyond, working evenings and weekends, I also realised that it was vital to keep some clear boundaries as burnout would be a possibility otherwise, which wouldn't be good for myself or the project.

Resilience to me is about keeping going and staying focused whatever the challenges in the way and believing in the achievability of the end goal.

[Results] Focusing upon resilience in my project ensured that I stayed on top of things and guided the project to a successful completion."

Competency Example – "Can You Give Us an Example Of When You Supported Change?"

This is a question that will occasionally surface for some roles.

As change is a given in the modern world, the interviewer will want to hear that you are comfortable with change and see it as a necessary and exciting part of working life.

Example

> *"Change is an important part of working life I think that it's really important to be flexible, as organisations work in an ever changing environment.*
>
> *I think a good example of when I supported change effectively was when a company I was working for had to deal with new legal regulations which completely changed the way that we worked, requiring completely new processes and paperwork [Situation]. Because this was a change in the law that was central to our work, it was vital to make the change quickly, as non-compliance could lead to problems for the company [Importance].*
>
> *I was part of a team dealing with customers, and the changes impacted our team directly [Task].*
>
> *Many of my colleagues were quite upset buy these changes and found them challenging. They were therefore initially slow to instigate the new processes, but I made sure that I understood what changes were required and set about dealing with them in the workplace as effectively and positively as possible [Actions].*

Although it did mean doing things in a completely different way with whole new set of paperwork it also did make some elements easier in the long run.

The paperwork was actually reduced under the new way of doing things so although it required completely relearning the process, once that was achieved there was considerable saving in time [Results].

I think when it comes to change it's important to engage with it rather than resisting it because change is necessary as organisations are working in a rapidly changing environment both in terms of competition and regulation."

Closing Questions for the Interviewers

At the end of the interview, it's quite normal and indeed expected for the candidate to ask questions of the interviewers. These questions are typically about the position, the organisation and so on.

It is important to have at least something to ask the interviewer, but it's much better if you don't overdo it. There is a fine line between showing a really positive interest in the position by asking incisive questions, or overwhelming the interviewer with too many, too obvious, or unanswerable questions. Sometimes the interviewer will just want to move on to discussing your interview with others on the panel, and the question to you is a courtesy…

Top Tip
- Have questions ready, but don't overdo the number of questions you ask.

So, lets take a look at some of the possibilities…

There are a few questions that you should consider asking. If it has been an in-depth interview, with discussion about the organisation and the position, if it is appropriate for the interview it can be useful to start with something on the lines of:

> *"Actually, I did have a few things I was unsure of, but we have answered most of those as we have gone along – thank you. However, there are a couple of questions that I would like to ask…"*

Then a couple of questions such as:

> • *"When should I hear from you, and what would the next steps be?"*

- *"If I was successful, how do you see this position developing over time?"*

- *"What would a typical day for someone in this position look like?"*

- *"What is your aim for the postholder in this position to achieve?"*

- *"What is the workplace culture like here?"*

This is a great way to round off your interview, showing interest in the position.

Top Tip
- Focus your questions about the position, looking forward.

After the Interview

Following the interview, you will probably walk out of the interview room feeling totally shattered! That's not surprising – those previous minutes have been highly stressful, and stress is highly draining.

Now, as you leave, don't forget to be pleasant to everyone, and thank the receptionist if there is one. Remember what we said earlier about everyone possibly having an input in terms of their impressions of you. Though you may not feel like it, that extra smile in place for a few moments more can sometimes pay off.

However, there are still things to be done. As soon as you reasonably can, send them and email thanking them for seeing you and that you are looking forward to hearing from them.

Then, all you can probably do for this interview is to wait for the outcome. How quickly you hear will depend on the organization and its recruitment process. I have encountered decisions being confirmed in timescales varying from at the end of the interview itself – that's pretty quick – to three months later (yes, three months!). Hopefully, you will have got an idea from the interview about the likely timescale.

However, while this interview is over, my own suggestion would be to begin to immediately prepare for the next interview. Now, that may seem very negative and pessimistic – surely there's a good chance the job will be yours if you have prepared well, but whilst that is indeed the case, there are no guarantees. Crucially the memory of the interview such as what you said and how you said it is far fresher in your mind now – just after the interview – than it will be when you try to remember later on. Even if you think you'll remember everything, you'll be surprised how quickly it fades, especially the important details.

So, whilst it is still all there in your mind take what you did today and reflect to start to decide areas of improvement to work on to be ready for your next interview. Having said that, our memory is a strange thing and it's not uncommon for people who have been under stress in the interview to forget almost everything the moment that they leave! If so, just work with whatever you can remember…

Jot down a few notes about what you felt you could do better, but also what you feel went well. This reflection is important, as however much preparation you have done, there is always something that crops up that you didn't expect and can learn from.

Now start that research for the next interview or continue it if you have got an interview already lined up. Make sure that your preparation is even better for next time. Interviews are a skill that can be learnt. There are no guarantees, but anything you can do that will tip the scales in your favour is certainly worth doing.

When you do hear back, there will hopefully be cause for much celebration about your new position. If, however, you have not been successful make sure that you ask for feedback as to why. If they don't offer it, then do ask for it, as they should really give it to you – again some organisations wont but the most professional ones usually will.

Look at the information they provide, was it your strengths of weaknesses? Was it a different aspect of your experience that they were looking for? Try to make sure you understand the gaps that you may have had so you can fill them ready to move forward. With this information, revisit relevant modules of this course to help you construct an even better interview technique.

Good luck – make sure that you prepare and ensure you give them the best interview they have ever seen!

Top Tips

- Send a follow-up email thanking them for seeing you.
- Reflect on what you could do better next time, whilst memory is fresh.
- Use any feedback from the interview fully.

Using Your Voice Effectively

Whenever you prepare for an interview, the first thing that you will usually consider is what you are going to say. However, there is another crucial element that most people don't think enough about, and that is just how you will say it. Yet the use of your voice - in terms of volume, pitch, emphasis, pace and the way you vary or modulate your voice – can help shape the interviewers' opinions about you.

Your voice is therefore a key tool in presenting yourself effectively in your interview and is an aspect that the interviewer will instantly form an impression of you from. It can be a core part of projecting confidence throughout the interview, and indeed, we pick up so many different aspects of personality and emotion through the voice that it's worth really exploring how we can make a difference by using it more effectively.

Think about your own experiences of hearing other people speak. Perhaps you might remember back to your college or University days – you may have had lecturers that could bring a subject alive through their enthusiasm and passion for their subject, whilst others could suck the life out of theirs by sounding boring or disinterested. Which would you rather sound like at interview?

As well as being able to gauge enthusiasm and interest from someone's voice, you can often tell how nervous someone is too, and as projecting confidence is so important, this is something else we need to consider.

There are several factors within how we speak – excluding the words themselves – that we can think about. These include:
- The volume of our voice.
- The pitch of our voice, which may be high, medium or low.
- The modulation or variation of the pitch.

- The pace, which can vary from really slow, to very fast.
- The emphasis on particular words or syllables…

Just think of a simple phrase consisting of two short sentences totalling nine words…

Are you sure? I think you might be mistaken…

How many ways could you change the intent and subtext of that simple sentence, just through changing *how* you say it? Emphasising different words, using different intonations such as sarcastic or empathic, can all change the underlying meaning…

Now, consider what happens to our voice when we are nervous. For a start our speaking rate tends to increase - often quite dramatically - when we are nervous or feel under pressure. If we are not careful, we start to gabble as if we are trying to get what we are saying out as quickly as possible. Because we are speaking so quickly our speech can sometimes overtake our brain and we can end up speaking faster than we can think. Before we know it, we are saying almost random things rather than the well-considered answers we want to deliver.

Secondly, our pitch can sometimes start to rise (sometimes dramatically), which doesn't sound good to the interviewer.

Thirdly, sometimes we can also reduce the volume we are speaking in, or fade out at the end of sentences making our answers hard to hear.

So, what to do? Naturally, the first thing we must suggest is to slow down if you are speaking too quickly. This will give a more confident impression and, as it's suggested by cognitive scientists that we can only take in information about 150 to 160 words per minute, by exceeding this were also actually overloading our interviewer who therefore cannot appreciate our answers!

A slower voice can often have also more power or authority. Think of somebody such as Winston Churchill who spoke slowly and with gravitas, and by doing so had an undeniable power in his speech. He also had a really distinctive use of intonation. OK, so you may not want to sound like Churchill, but you get the idea. Don't speak too fast…

Remember, the pitch of our voice tends to rise when we are nervous. Think about the impression that could give the interviewer, when they see someone who sounds like they've just inhaled a balloon of helium before entering the room. What we want to put across is confidence, which is usually more about having a lower voice.

So, to sound confident, tending to a lower pitch and slower pacing would be the way to go to counteract the natural tendencies to speed up and rise. Remember – lower and slower…. However, again don't overdo it. Don't sound too slow and boring. Notice your voice and slow it down and lower it if you are starting to gabble and speed up too much. Also, make sure that you speak clearly and loudly enough, but don't overdo the volume.

However, that doesn't mean that this is the only strategy – low, good pace and loud enough is a fairly safe bet and can help to keep nerves in check.

However, for some people, depending on their personality, sometimes going the other way and using a lot of pace and modulating your voice can be effective. Doing this puts across passion and can draw the interviewer into your excitement. Provided you can speak quickly and effectively, while still maintaining clarity, carefully considering what you're saying, constructing good answers and not overloading the interviewer it can have a very strong influential effect. An example of this way of speaking was the late astronomy populariser Patrick Moore, who in his prime spoke very rapidly but clearly, and with a distinctive diction.

Record yourself giving an answer to a possible interview question, and listen back. How do you sound? What impression will that give?

Top Tips
- One key way of sounding confident is to talk more slowly, and with lower pitch.
- Alternatively, an animated passionate voice can work well.

One other important element of the use of voice that people often fail to do, is to ensure that there are short pauses or breaks between different sections of your answer. When I'm coaching clients, I find that at first, they often speak without a break. Doing this can make it more difficult for the interviewer to really absorb and understand what you are saying, especially when one topic we are talking about continues into another.

These pauses only need to be very brief, but make sure that they are in there. For example, if you are telling the interviewer about your strengths, running them together without pause can be unclear, so a very short pause between each to clearly delineate them can help make your answer sound clearer and more structured.

One other important element that we often forget or don't use in pressured situations is longer silences. We tend to be afraid of leaving gaps in what we say, and yet it can be a powerful tool, giving you time to think and for your listener to absorb information. It can also give a feeling that you are in control of the situation. Taking a few moments before you answer, or even during it, can be effective in allowing you to think about and structure your answer.

You have to consider carefully what style of speaking is going to most of you and your interviews. Can you speak with passion and quickly and clearly enough to put that enthusiasm across without overloading the interview panel? Or are you better off speaking slowly and in a more measured and powerful way? There is, as ever, no absolute, but is an important thing to consider before the interview itself, and even practice using your voice to understand how it sounds and what it puts across.

Top Tips
- Ensure you have short breaks between the sections of your answer - running them together can lose clarity.
- Record your voice on your phone etc., answering a question as you would in interview. Then listen back and consider your voice.
- Think about what you hear:
  o Are you clear?
  o Are you speaking too quickly, or too slowly?
  o Do you sound confident?
  o Is your voice animated?

Body Language

In an interview there are many things that contribute to the overall impression that the interviewer will form of you. One of the most important is your body language, from which your interviewer will pick up a lot about you and how confident you are. This means that understanding and using it can make a big difference.

There are many elements to body language – it's a complex topic - so we'll concentrate on the key ones that are easiest to work with and which can make a big difference…

So, what are the most important elements of body language to use in an interview?…

Posture

The first element to consider is posture – specifically whether our posture is oriented up or down. This up/down direction is important in the impression that we put across to others, especially in terms of confidence. For example, think about when you are sad or depressed – what do you do? You tend to hunch and look down. When you lack confidence, you do the same.

Now consider your body language when you are feeling good, really happy and confident – what do you do then? You look upwards… Indeed, to celebrate a great success we may not only look up but might even put our hands up in the air - consider a footballer who has just scored a goal or an athlete winning a race, head up and arms high up in the air. Admittedly, going into your interview with your hands in the air might be over the top, but as our confidence and positive feelings are conveyed by this up/down direction - up for positive, down for negative - you want to have an upright posture, and with your head up, and certainly not hunched and looking down at the desk…

So, in the interview, remember, are you looking up at the panel or down at the desk? Is your torso upright, or are you hunched over? Use that first aspect of your body language to communicate confidence…

Open Body Language

One of the classic elements that you will also see in all the texts about body language is whether your body language is open or closed. Do you have your arms folded, demonstrating closed body language and seemingly shutting yourselves off from others, or are they open which is more inviting of interaction?

The idea is that closed body language, such as folding your arms, is defensive and you can understand why, as folding our arms does form a physical barrier between you and the other person.

Closed body language should be avoided.

You want to ensure that your body language is open, so don't fold your own arms - the interviewer may take it as defensive and closed off which is not what you wish to put across. Open body language is much more powerful.

Something else to keep in mind is that we also read others body language, and sometimes we might get the wrong idea... Your interviewer, especially one on a panel not asking the question, may have their arms folded. There is a danger here that you notice and think that they have switched off, or aren't interested in you and what you are saying. This can throw you off your game, and even make you try increasingly wild ways of re-engaging them. However, many people fold their arms not to be defensive and closed off, but because they may just be more comfortable that way – it's important not to take others folded arms as a negative signal.

So don't fold your own arms as others may read this as defensive and closed off, but also don't assume that the panel have stopped listening to you and disengaged just because they have their arms folded. It may not be the case...

The Smile

An obvious aspect of body language you really want to use to good effect is your smile. Smiling appropriately in interviews is good. It shows we are confident and that's what we want to project. Be aware, though, that there are two types of smile...

Firstly there is the genuine and natural smile, called the 'Duchenne' smile after the wonderfully named 19th century neurologist Guillaume-Benjamin-Amand Duchenne (de Boulogne). He was the first to investigate and understand the ways in different muscle groups in and around the face work together to form a natural smile.

The other smile is often known as the Pan Am smile. Pan Am was Pan American, an airline that went out of business in December

1991. The Pan Am smile is an artificial smile – imagine if you will, flight attendants greeting those boarding the plane and having to constantly generate a smile however they may really feel inside.

The difference between them isn't in the mouth – they tend to be much the same between both. Instead, the difference is in the eyes – or rather beside them. When we are genuinely happy or amused, the muscles by our eyes tend to crinkle the skin there. When we give a false smile, they simply do not. You might get away with a small false-ish smile, but don't try to overdo it as too big a smile will be obviously fake. This is why you can instinctively feel when a smile is false – if you want to get a good feel for this, just take a look at pictures of actresses and actors smiling on the red carpet and see if you can spot the difference.

Naturally, in an interview, you want to use a smile to really connect with the interviewer and show a sense of confidence and positivity. Try to make it a genuine smile of pleasure at being considered for the position and having the opportunity to talk to the interviewer about why you are the right person for the job. Don't give too big a smile if you aren't feeling it, but certainly don't look grumpy!…

Eye Contact

Eye contact can be a very intense signal. It is a sign of confidence and/or dominance. When we are nervous or under pressure from another person (such as our interviewer) we tend to look away from them, so maintaining a good level of eye contact and using it to engage with the interviewer can really create a powerful impression of being confident and feeling in control of the situation.

However, don't overdo it. If you stare hard at your interviewer for too long, it can be somewhat disconcerting! Think of how you feel when someone stares for too long at you – it can seem a worrying, hostile, or just weird! Therefore, the best thing to do is to vary your eye contact, looking at the interviewer for most of the time, but occasionally looking away. In a panel interview, varying eye contact by looking at different members of the panel gives you a chance to vary it by switching between people, yet maintain a good level of eye contact overall. Make sure that most of your attention is on the interviewer who has asked you the question, and then look to the others occasionally to engage and include them.

I mention in the section about interview types that in a panel interview, different interviewers may have different roles. Often there will be a senior person who will actually make the final decision, based upon input from the others who may, for instance, include a specialist and an HR person. If you get a feel that someone is more senior in an interview, ensure that they get a good amount of eye contact during your answers, even if they aren't the person asking the question. Show your respect for them, but don't leave the others out – no-one likes to be ignored.

For anyone who likes acronyms to help them remember, one you could use here is POSE!

This stands for Posture, Open, Smile and Eyes:
'P' for your upright **Posture**
'O' for using **Open** body language
'S' for a genuine **Smile**
'E' for good modulated **Eye Contact**

Top Tips
- Remember 'POSE'
  - 'P' for your upright Posture
  - 'O' for using Open body language
  - 'S' for a genuine Smile
  - 'E' for good modulated Eye Contact

Animation

One last thing to think about – animation. Some people are naturally very animated and use their arms and hands to gesture and as part of their explanation. In interviews, it might be thought that it's better to be more controlled and less animated. However, I don't agree that that is always the case. If you are someone who is natural expressive and animated, trying to really shut this down can be disconcerting and feel unnatural to you, possibly getting in the way of you feeling relaxed and delivering in an engaging way. I think that being animated (within reason) can communicate a passion and an excitement which is really valuable!

So, if you are someone who uses gestures when they talk – that is probably fine

Confidence and Mindset, An Introduction

In an interview, as in many areas of life and work, confidence sells – not over-confidence but instead a natural feeling of assurance. It's powerful and it works because people take confidence to equate with competence, which is the impression we want to create. This confidence can come from having the right mindset.

Interview Anxiety

Nerves and anxiety are common when facing interviews - indeed, one could almost say that they are almost universal. Whether I'm working with those just starting their careers or high-flying executives, it's still an issue that emerges most of the time… Therefore, I'd like to start by reminding you of the reassuring point that you won't be the first person to be nervous in an interview, and you certainly won't be the last either. Other applicants for the post will probably be as nervous as you, as I can virtually guarantee that everyone else going for the same position as you will lack inner confidence in some way…

Actually, having some interview nerves isn't always a bad thing. Without the presence of some nerves, we can be too laid back and so appear over-confident, which doesn't project well. We also know that a certain amount of stress can actually help us focus and perform optimally, as research has shown that in terms of the relationship between stress and performance, our performance is weakest at both very high and very low stress levels, and peaks where there is just enough tension to give us that edge that we need.

But that is the key – just enough tension. For obvious reasons we don't want the stress to become overwhelming. If it does, not only do we not project the right image, but we can dry up in the middle of an interview as our mind goes blank.

To deal with stress effectively, I think that it helps to understand a little about how our response to stress works, so let's consider what is known as the 'flight or fight' response.

Understanding Stress - Fight or Flight

'Flight or Fight' (sometimes also known as flight, fight, or freeze) is our bodies natural response to a stressful situation. It has origins that go way back to deep in our evolutionary past as thousands of years ago, we faced all sorts of real and immediate threats to our very existence - physical threats and that had to be met with a physical response.

This response involved changes occurring within our bodies that were designed to allow us to do one of two things - either physically fighting the threat or running away from it – 'flight' or 'fight'.

To achieve this, firstly adrenaline is pumped into our system to get it primed and ready to go, and our heart rate increases to force blood and oxygen around our body to fuel our muscles ready for physical action. Our breathing changes to shorter rapid breaths, and a burst of extra fuel is released into the body in the form of sugars to give us energy. Meanwhile, our internal digestive organs tend to slow down as blood flow shifts away from them to instead carry oxygen to the essential muscles in our arms and legs etc.

There are also important cognitive shifts in the way that we think, that can affect us, but we'll discuss this later.

Now this is a well-honed and very powerful way of dealing with any real physical threats to our existence, and we probably wouldn't be here today if it wasn't effective. But job interviews (however it may feel to us) aren't really 'life or death' situations, so why is this response important to understand?

It is because it is a natural and powerful response to a stressor – any stressor – and this includes interviews! Therefore, our body can respond to an interview the same way that thousands of years ago we responded to a potentially lethal encounter....

So, what will happen to us as we approach and enter the interview, and what could be problematic? Well, we will feel the adrenaline flowing round our system, which can make us feel 'pumped up' – perhaps shaky or jumpy. We may feel our increased blood flow pumping as our heart pounding away more rapidly in our chests. The change in blood flow round our bodies and change in blood pressure also means we may flush red...

This is one of the reasons too much coffee beforehand can be a problem – you are already hyped up enough without caffeine joining the party and making you even jumpier... The blood flowing away from our internal organs to the muscles means that our stomach can feel unsettled – we get butterflies in our stomach or even worse problems with our digestive system in extreme cases. That's not great!

Also, I mentioned earlier that the mind itself undergoes a cognitive shift when we are stressed. There is a narrowing down of the focus of our thoughts by concentrating upon the perceived threat pretty much to the exclusion of everything else. Logically, this makes sense, as you can imagine that if you were faced with an enemy then being distracted and looking at, say, the pretty flowers all around you instead of the focussing upon the threat is not going to be a great survival strategy...

However, in the interview room this means a focus upon the worries of the interview situation. This is one of the reasons that our mind can go blank – we are consumed with thinking about what might go wrong, leaving less brain capacity to think through our answers. We can also be so consumed with the worry that we don't really listen to the questions, which can naturally cause all sorts of difficulties for us.

This means that developing confidence and reducing our stress levels is therefore crucially important, so let's begin to explore what we can do to achieve this - we will first take a look at ways of reducing interview stress and anxiety directly, and then move into confidence and mindset...

Breathing for Calmness

One of the most powerful ways of overcoming the flight or fight stress response is to use breathing exercises. These can be used almost anywhere and anytime, especially in the lead-up to interview day and while you are sitting waiting for the interview.

We need to adopt the breathing pattern and technique that is associated with relaxation and calmness to relax our bodies and allow our minds to recover balance. The following assumes that you have a healthy respiratory system. If you don't, check with your doctor first before commencing any breathing exercise.

Now, I must mention that most people do find breathing exercises really relaxing and help them destress. However, they don't suit everybody, and so if you find it that focussing upon your breathing actually makes you more anxious, then just stop – it doesn't happen often, but can do for some people.

Something else to be aware of, is that especially when starting out on a breathing exercise for the first time, that you may begin to feel quite light headed. If so, just open your eyes again and allow your breathing to return to normal – it means that this new breathing pattern is taking in more oxygen which your body is not used to. Give yourself a while to return to normal, and then try again but more cautiously this time, and again stopping if the light-headedness returns. Over time your body will usually get used to it and you'll be able to breathe more effectively without feeling lightheaded, but do take it carefully.

A Destressing Beathing Exercise

This is a simple but powerful breathing exercise that can really help you to destress. After some minutes of doing it correctly, this breathing exercise can make you feel really relaxed.

- Firstly, notice where you are breathing from. Sometimes we breathe from our diaphragm ('belly breathing') and sometimes we breathe from higher up in our chest ('chest breathing'). Ideally, we should 'belly breathe', as by doing so it helps us to relax and rid ourselves of stress. So, if you are chest breathing, try to shift to breathing from lower in your torso - 'belly breathing' instead. Get that diaphragm moving!.

- Breathe in through your nose, and out through your mouth.

- Breathe fully, but don't overdo it.

- Breathe as smoothly as you can.

- This is the crucial bit — take at least twice as long to breathe out as to breathe in. So, if you breathe in for a count of 4, then breathe out for at least a count of 8.

- This can relax quickly. However, if calming nerves before the day, try to do this exercise for 15 minutes (or more) to really gain maximum benefit.

A Confident Interview Mindset

There is a saying - 'what is expected, tends to be realised'. It means that things tend to go the way we think that they will, because we make it a self-fulfilling prophecy. If we expect to be nervous in an interview, clam up with a blank mind, and forget everything that we had planned to say, then that is far more likely to happen. If, on the other hand, we expect to be confident and be able to answer the interviewers probing questions easily and with assurance, then that is the scenario is more likely to play out.

This would suggest that we need to set up a mindset of an expectation of success, confidence, and competence at interview. So how can we go about this? Well, research suggests that our mind doesn't view imagined experiences and real ones that differently. This suggests that if we imagine ourselves going through successful interviews, we are creating an inner set of positive expectations that our subconscious can draw upon when we get to the real thing.

This is the basis of imagination rehearsal, a technique used in many areas of endeavour and excellence including athletes, business people and executives, and other high performers. By carefully preparing in your mind, you can ready yourself to be calmer and more positive and effective in the interview.

Let's explore some mindset exercises you can use. Please note that, as with other suggested exercises, these mindset exercise should only be when you have the ability to focus upon it completely. It should under no circumstances be done whilst driving etc.

Now, before you do the exercise, I would like to introduce it by exploring what thoughts and expectations about your interview performance are in your mind already…

So, think about the forthcoming interview. If you haven't got a specific one lined up, that's ok, just focus upon what you expect when one does arise. Think of yourself in that interview, facing the interviewer, answering their questions…

Become aware of how you feel it might go - you can almost think of it as a movie playing in the inner cinema of your mind. On one level, we can consciously think to ourselves that everything will be fine, whilst our subconscious has other ideas – and it's the subconscious imagery that can have the greatest effect. So, you might be consciously telling yourself that you will perform perfectly, whilst less helpful images that bubble up from deep down in your subconscious mean that you are also aware of seeing everything going horribly wrong!

Indeed, you may find, as you become aware of your thoughts and expectations, that your subconscious has catastrophised things by imagining things going really badly wrong – perhaps being unable to think to what to say, or giving a disastrously bad answer. If so, be aware that this is really quite common and it's this deep negative image that we need to change, which is what the following exercise is all about...

Top Tip
- Use an Imagination Rehearsal Exercise

Imagination Rehearsal Exercise

Our first exercise is a straightforward imagination rehearsal. If you are going to use this, give yourself plenty of time and don't rush it - it can be powerful but only if done correctly. Try it several times on the run-up to your interview to enhance the effect.

Read through the following instructions, and then give it a go...

Close your eyes and imagine as well as you can the interview that you would like to perform well in, seeing yourself from the 3rd person perspective. Make sure in your imagination you look positive and confident and deliver excellent answers - you're creating the blueprint of how you would like to perform within the interview so ensure that the imagery is positive.

Go through the stages of the interview, seeing yourself from the 3rd person perspective, and being positive and confident.

- See yourself approaching the interview, either going online or walking into the venue.
- Waiting for the interview to start – seeing your calmness and confidence.
- Greeting the interviewers, smiling, building rapport.
- Answering questions easily, even the tricky ones
- Finishing the interview and asking them questions.
- Leaving the interview

Now, repeat this, but this time it's from the 1st person, seeing things as if through your own eyes.

- Imagine you are preparing for the interview, either going online or walking into the venue.

- Waiting for the interview to start – feeling your calmness and confidence.
- Greeting the interviewers, smiling, building rapport.
- Answering questions easily, even the tricky ones
- Finishing the interview and asking them questions.
- Leaving the interview

By doing this, you are creating an expectation of confidence in your mind, for you to draw on within the interview.

This exercise should be repeated several times in the run-up to the interview.

Inner Dialogue

Imagine now you are walking into your next interview... What are you saying to yourself as you do so? Are you telling yourself that it's going to go well, or that it's going to be a disaster?

You see, we all have that inner voice - our inner thoughts - that tells us what we are thinking. It often comments on what we have done, or alternatively how things will go! This is not a hallucinated voice that can be associated with mental health issues, but is part of the natural thought processes that we all have within us...

Many years ago, psychologists tended to think that our inner dialogue reflected and was driven by our feelings, so that it if we felt worried then our inner dialogue would start telling us negative things. Yet it seems that it is usually the other way round – what our inner voice says to us, shapes our emotions - confidence or anxiety.

To illustrate this, try an interesting but perhaps somewhat surreal exercise. If you are aware of a negative inner voice, perhaps telling you that your interview won't go well, for a few moments, to change that inner voice to a funny one. Perhaps, if you remember it, the Swedish Chef from the old Muppet Show can be a good choice – the character who talked nonsense in mock Swedish.

Now, how does that feel?

Most people find that, when they are running the Swedish Chef inner voice, they actually feel different. Usually, they can't take the voice as seriously, and this can quickly change their feelings to much lighter, even humorous.

Now I'm not saying that you should go around with the Swedish Chef as your inner voice all the time! However, it does demonstrate the power that this inner voice has to affect us, and it suggests that by changing our inner voice we could actually change how we feel and do so quite quickly. So, think again about interviews. As you are walking into the interview, what would you want to be saying to yourself?

You can explore working with your inner voice by doing the inner dialogue exercise. It can help you develop more confidence for your interview.

Inner Dialogue Exercise

<u>**Stage 1**</u>

Take a few moments to think about the next interview you will go to - whether you have a specific one lined up or not doesn't matter, just think about the next one you imagine it could be if you haven't got one arranged.

Notice what you are silently telling yourself about it in your mind?

Note whether you are telling yourself 'It's going to go really well' or alternatively "I'm really worried about the interview. My mind will go blank. I'll be terrible".

Notice, now, how you are feeling about this interview.

Think how your inner dialogue and your inner feelings relate to each other?

<u>Stage 2</u>

Create some inner dialogue that is really powerful and positive, such as:

> *"I can do it".*
>
> *"I'm going to deliver a great interview".*
>
> *"I am confident and positive".*

Try this for a few moments, and notice how it feels…

<u>Stage 3</u>

Practice this inner dialogue repeatedly as you run up to the interview.

<u>Stage 4</u>

If, on interview day, you need a confidence boost, run this positive inner dialogue.

It's important to make the inner dialogue positive, and not about negating negatives. To explain, for the brain to react to the statement 'I am not anxious' it has to access the concept of anxiety to understand what you are saying!

That's not what you want – instead of thinking about anxiety you want those neurons of yours to be processing the concept of confidence and calmness… So, it's important to say "I am confident" rather than "I am not anxious" or "I am calm" rather than "I am not stressed" …

The Appendices

I hope that you have gained some useful tips from reading this book. It was my intention to try to put across as many helpful ideas as I could in an accessible format.

The appendices following include a couple of more advanced ideas. They aren't for everyone, but if you are experienced at interviews and/or are going for a senior position, they might be useful to consider.

Don't forget that there are also more resources at my website:

www.interviewsuccess.uk

Appendix 1 - COSY

In many interviews, especially when answering competency questions, you will find it important to give your answers in such a way that demonstrates consideration of different perspectives. For this, the acronym COSY can be useful.

The C is for Colleagues, that is your colleagues, team, team members, etc. This can include other teams within the organisation (although they may also sometimes be considered as stakeholders, depending on the situation) as the key element is you are demonstrating awareness of impacts for those around you.

The O is for the Organisation. This is how your actions affect the organisation as an entity – particularly with respect to the bigger picture and the outside world. Hence its perception, reputation, profitability etc.

The S is the Service Users. These can be Customers, Clients, Patients, Stakeholders, or other Service Users. In effect this is who you and/or the organisation is there for. Usually considered to be outside the organisation for the purposes of this approach.

Finally, the 'Y' is You! How this affected you. By the way, if you prefer, you could use 'I' and make it COSI – it's entirely up to you!

Probably the best way of explaining this more fully is to look at part of an example answer...

'I had a situation where our customer was really annoyed and getting rapidly angrier. I was aware that if I didn't deal with this effectively, it was likely that other team members would get involved which would take them away from their work for other customers (C) and had the possibility of escalating onto social media, which could mean that the reputational impact on our

company could be severe (O). Also, I really wanted to make sure that the customer was happy, and I felt that he had a valid grievance (S) so I felt it important to handle it myself as although I was really busy and had another meeting pressing, it was more important to deal with this immediately (You or I). "

Hopefully, you can see how this gives a different perspective that is better than just a focus on yourself and what you did. You are thinking of the bigger picture – a skill that many interviewers are looking for.

Appendix 2 –SPIDAR(R)

Earlier, we reviewed replacing STAR with SITAR. However, there may be times that you might want to deliver answers with an even more detailed structure, and a good approach here is SPIDAR(R).

SPIDAR(R) can work well in more advanced interviews for senior roles in organisations, where a broader awareness and deeper response is required. It is designed to demonstrate more about your thought or decision process, which can be important for really impressing your interviewer.

SPIDAR stands for:
- S Situation – The situation that occurred.
- P Position – Your position, or role.
- I Importance – Why was it important?
- D Decision Process - What were your thoughts and ideas. What process did you use to make the decision? What did you consider?
- A Action – What you actually did
- R Result – The result of your actions,
- (R) Reflection – (Optional)Reflection on what worked and what didn't - What would you do next time?

You can perhaps see where things get a bit different from the STAR or SITAR approach. The D is the decision process you used to decide your course of action, and the extra D step gives a chance to demonstrate your thinking, which can be important.

There is also another additional letter which is another 'R' to make the acronym SPIDARR. This R is for Reflection – reflecting upon what worked, and what didn't, and what you would do differently next time. It demonstrates personal and professional growth and experience but should only be used where you feel it would add to your answer.

Let's see this in action in a brief example:

"In my previous career there was an extremely tight deadline for an important project (Situation). I was team leader, and so my role was to make sure that the project got delivered on time, and also met the brief we had been given (Position). This project was important to the organisation as it would really raise our profile and so enable us to win more key clients, which would allow us to expand both in terms of market sector and also into new markets (Importance). I looked at the situation and considered whether we had the resources, in terms of people, that we needed and decided that we had, but I also realised that using everyone in the team optimally would be vital (Decision Process). So, in order to make sure that we hit the deadline I broke down what we needed to do and distributed it between the team members based on what I saw to be their skills and experience, so each could focus upon one section and so make sure that it was completed on time (Action). Doing this meant that we actually managed to complete the project within the overall time frame and still keep it under budget overall. (Result).

Though we completed it successfully, I realised afterwards that it was dependent upon everyone achieving their tasks, and if a team member had gone off sick or was unavailable, that would have caused problems. In a similar future situation, I would try to ensure some extra resources in terms of team members to make sure that a critical project like this is delivered successfully 100% of the time. (Reflection)".

This is a great structure for a broad answer that highlights key aspects of you and how you work.

Why not try it out and see if it helps you to create a detailed and yet structured answer.

Mike Culley C.Psychol. AFBPsS

Mike Culley is an occupational psychologist, with a background in enhancing individual workplace performance, and applying practical psychology solutions to real-world situations.

He has conducted selection and interviews extensively for a range of different organisations, and coached clients both within the UK and from around the World to enhance their interview skills and help them to secure their new positions.

His website is at **www.interviewsuccess.uk**

www.ingramcontent.com/pod-product-compliance
Lightning Source LLC
Chambersburg PA
CBHW070341220526
45467CB00001B/199